# This Sumptuous Church

# This Sumptuous Church
## THE STORY OF DURHAM CATHEDRAL

## C. J. STRANKS

London

SPCK

1973

First published in 1973
by SPCK
Holy Trinity Church
Marylebone Road
London NW1 4DU


Printed in Great Britain by
Northumberland Press Ltd, Gateshead

SBN 281 02751 X

*To The Dean*
*and Chapter of Durham*
*my colleagues*
*through many happy years*

# Contents

## 1 *The Middle Ages*

## 2 *The Reformation*

# 3 The Eighteenth Century and After

# List of Illustrations

ix

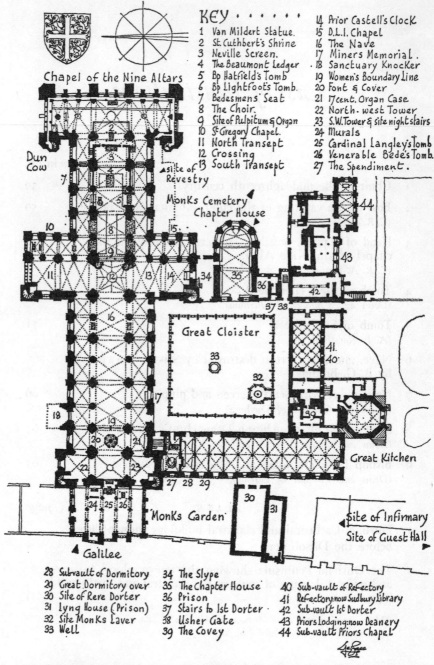

KEY . . . . . .
1 Van Mildert Statue.
2 St. Cuthbert's Shrine.
3 Neville Screen.
4 The Beaumont Ledger
5 Bp Hatfield's Tomb
6 Bp Lightfoot's Tomb.
7 Bedesmens' Seat
8 The Choir.
9 Site of Pulpitum & Organ
10 St Gregory Chapel.
11 North Transept
12 Crossing
13 South Transept

14 Prior Castell's Clock
15 D.L.I. Chapel
16 The Nave
17 Miners Memorial.
18 Sanctuary Knocker
19 Women's Boundary Line
20 Font & Cover
21 17cent. Organ Case
22 North-west Tower
23 S.W.Tower & site night stairs
24 Murals
25 Cardinal Langley's Tomb
26 Venerable Bede's Tomb.
27 The Spendiment.

Chapel of the Nine Altars

Dun Cow

site of Revestry

Monks Cemetery

Chapter House

Great Cloister

Great Kitchen

Monks Garden

Site of Infirmary
Site of Guest Hall

Galilee

28 Subvault of Dormitory
29 Great Dormitory over
30 Site of Rere Dorter
31 Lyng House (Prison)
32 Site Monks Laver
33 Well

34 The Slype
35 The Chapter House
36 Prison
37 Stairs to 1st Dorter
38 Usher Gate
39 The Covey

40 Sub-vault of Refectory
41 Refectory now Sudbury Library
42 Sub-vault 1st Dorter
43 Priors Lodging now Deanery
44 Sub-vault Priors Chapel

Durham Cathedral and claustral buildings showing use before the Dissolution

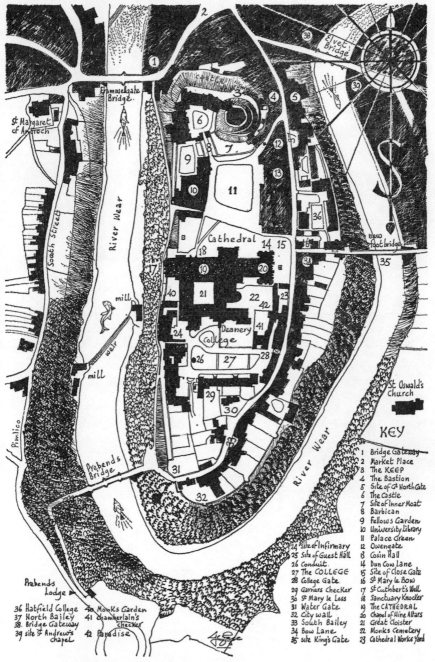

Map of the Durham Peninsula showing the topographical features and present day use of some of the claustral and castle buildings

**KEY**

1. Bridge Gateway
2. Market Place
3. The KEEP
4. The Bastion
5. Site of G<sup>t</sup> North Gate
6. The Castle
7. Site of Inner Moat
8. Barbican
9. Fellows Garden
10. University Library
11. Palace Green
12. Owengate
13. Cosin Hall
14. Dun Cow Lane
15. Site of Close Gate
16. St Mary le Bow
17. St Cuthbert's Well
18. Sanctuary Knocker
19. The CATHEDRAL
20. Chapel of Nine Altars
21. Great Cloister
22. Monks Cemetery
23. Cathedral Works Yard
24. Site of Infirmary
25. Site of Guest Hall
26. Conduit
27. The COLLEGE
28. College Gate
29. Garners Checker
30. St Mary le Less
31. Water Gate
32. City wall
33. South Bailey
34. Bow Lane
35. site King's Gate
36. Hatfield College
37. North Bailey
38. Bridge Gateway
39. site S<sup>t</sup> Andrew's chapel
40. Monks Garden
41. Chamberlain's checker
42. Paradise

# *Preface*

Durham Cathedral has a rich and splendid history. Its position, as the centre of a Prince Bishoprick of great wealth and power which was almost a separate kingdom, on the borders of England and Scotland, gives it a special place in our history. Its riches and importance have attracted to it throughout the centuries a series of vivid personalities who were, many of them, great national figures. Architecturally the cathedral may claim to be the finest example of Norman church building in England. Its religious life in all its various changes has been an epitome of the religious life of the whole country. As a centre of learning itself, and as the founder of great educational institutions it has served not only its own locality, but a great part of the world beside. An historian, wishing to deal with this, has at his disposal a vast mass of material, both printed and in manuscript, which gives a picture of nearly one thousand years of colourful and dramatic life.

One of the many advantages of living among a group of learned men is the help one receives, both from daily association with them, and from answers to specific questions, put to specific persons. I am enormously indebted to my brethren of the chapter in both these respects, though they cannot be held responsible for any errors of mine. Mr R. Norris, the dean and chapter's assistant librarian, has been tireless in finding the material I asked for, and Mr M. G. Snape, of the University's Department of Palaeography, gave me help with a number of medieval documents. Canon Charles Pattinson, the precentor, a friend of many years, drew my attention to items of interest in the chapter minutes and read the proofs. To these, and to many others too numerous to mention, I express my thanks.

*Durham*  C. J. STRANKS
*February 1973*

This reverend aged Abby is seated in the heart of the Citty, advanced upon the shoulders of an high Hill, and encompassed againe with the higher Hills, that he that hath seene the situation of this Citty, hath seene the Map of Sion, and may save a Journey to the Jerusalem. Shee is girded almost rownd with the renouned River of Weer, in which, as in a Glasse of Crystal, shee might once have beheld the beauty, but nowe the ruine of her Walls. To this sumptuous Church, was the last and great Translation of St Cuthbert.

ROBERT HEGG
*The Legend of St Cuthbert* (1626)

# 1

# *The Middle Ages*

## 1

## PILGRIMS OF FAITH

On an autumn day, in the year 995, a band of monks escorting a
bier emerged on to the rocky plateau lying in the bend of the river,
where Durham Cathedral now stands. With them were their cattle
and all their belongings, for they were migrating in search of a
home. The heavy coffin which they so closely guarded contained the
body of St Cuthbert, the greatest saint in the North Country, and
indeed in all England at that time. As a shepherd boy on the hills
outside Edinburgh, he had seen a vision of the soul of St Aidan
being carried to heaven by the angels, which had determined him
to become a monk. In the disciplined life of a Celtic monastery of
that day he had become famous for learning and holiness; so much
so that in 685, much against his will, he was made bishop of Lindisfarne, the island where his favourite monastery was situated. After
two years of missionary and pastoral work throughout Northumbria,
feeling that his end was near, he had retired to a solitary life on the
Great Farne Island, and there he died in 687.[1]

He was buried on Lindisfarne. When the body was examined
again, in 698, it was found to be undecayed. He had been very
emaciated when he died, and there can have been little left on his
body to decay; what remained was perhaps mummified by the salt
sand of his grave. So unexpected and wonderful a discovery was
proclaimed as a miracle, and his shrine became a centre of pilgrimage
from all over England. His popularity was no doubt helped by the
fact that, though he had been brought up in the old Celtic ways, he
accepted the Roman system in 664, and so appealed to both sides in
that controversy. When the Danish raiders came in 875, the monks of
Lindisfarne took their saint's body, and wandered with it in search
of safety. Everywhere the great sanctity of St Cuthbert and the fame
of his uncorrupt body brought adoring crowds and lavish gifts. For

1

107 years it rested in a wooden cathedral at Chester-le-Street, where the remains of the old Roman defences offered some protection from attack. In 995 renewed fears of the Danes set the monks wandering again, and after a few months' stay at Ripon, they turned northward, and came to Durham. It is unlikely that they arrived there by chance. The ancient Roman road from Piercebridge to Chester-le-Street, with which they must have been familiar, passed a little to the west of the loop in the Wear, which almost surrounded a rocky, tree-clad height and formed an obviously strong position. There was perhaps another consideration. Aldhun, their bishop, like some other Saxon bishops, was a married man. His daughter was the wife of Uchtred, the son and afterwards the heir, of the Earl of Northumberland, and had been dowered with church lands; which suggests that the connection was to be of benefit to the community. At Durham they would be under Uchtred's protection.[2] In later days, the legend grew up that the saint himself in a vision, had told his followers to settle in the Dunholme, the site of which they discovered by hearing a milkmaid speak of it as the place where a lost cow had strayed.

There had already been some occupation of the Peninsula before they arrived, for the centre had been cleared and partially cultivated; though all the rest was still covered with thick woodland, which spread down the steep banks to the river below. Their first care was to put up a rough hut of interlacing boughs to shelter the coffin. This was quickly replaced by a slightly better structure of wattle and daub, which was to last until the community had settled down and a worthy church could be built. To help them do this Uchtred impressed the whole population between the rivers Coquet and Tees, though little compulsion would be needed for so pious a work.[3] They cleared the whole site, and gave what help they could with the building. By 999 enough was finished for the church to be consecrated and the saint's body enshrined within it, on 4 September, though owing to marauding parties of Danes and Scots it was not completed until 1017. It was built of stone, and probably it was the bright newness of the work which won it the title of the White Church. There were two towers, one over the choir and the other at the West End and each was topped with a brass pinnacle. It was reckoned a marvellous building.

The monks who served it were not a very closely disciplined order. They seem to have been more a religious clan than a monastic community. The monks lived in houses of their own; many were married, and there were children among them, as the bones, discovered in their burial ground when the foundations at the East End of the present chapter house were opened up in 1874, were to prove. But slack as they might be, they expected their bishop to live a stricter life; consequently they had difficulty in finding men to accept the office. He lived among them, ruling both the community and the diocese from the same place and having no property that was distinguishable from theirs. Slight as it was, something like the religious life was being kept alive. About the year 1022 they had a sacrist called Elfrid Westoue who was very worried about the way in which the relics of the saints throughout Northumbria were being neglected; so he made it his business to seek them out, and bring as many as possible to Durham, where they could be properly cared for. Whether he thought Jarrow particularly vulnerable to heathen raiders, or whether he just coveted the relics it is hard to say; but after making several pilgrimages there on the anniversary of Bede's death and gaining the monks' trust, he made off early one morning with Bede's bones and said nothing to anybody about taking them, though when asked where they were, he would say that they would be found in the same coffin with those of St Cuthbert.[4] Such a famous possession as the uncorrupt body of St Cuthbert brought pilgrims from all over England, and every pilgrim brought his gift. Among them came King Canute and his retinue from their camp at Trimdon, with a royal gift of large tracts of land.

2

# THE NORMAN CONQUEST

England had been plagued long enough with the battles of Saxons, Danes, and Norwegians, but in 1066 William the Norman brought them to an end with his own strong rule. After reducing the south, he sent Robert Cumin with 700 men to take possession of the North-East. But it was not to be as easy as that. The population rose *en masse*, surrounded Durham, and at daybreak burst into the city, slaughtered every Norman in sight, and setting fire to the house where Cumin was lodging, burned him to death. It was said that only one of his seven hundred escaped. The two great earls, Edwin and Morcar, rebelled against William, were forgiven, and rebelled again, this time with help from the Vikings of Denmark. William himself therefore came North, and left his ferocious mark there. Every house between York and Durham was destroyed, and every

3

human being whom his soldiers could catch was slaughtered. Those who could get out of his way fled across the Tyne; though since they were robbed of all their possessions, they escaped to nothing more than slavery. The bishop and the Congregation of St Cuthbert shared in the general panic and hurriedly withdrew to Lindisfarne, taking the body of their saint with them. When they got there, they were dismayed to find that they were cut off by the sea, for they had no boat. So they prayed and waited, and in the morning they discovered that there was a way open to them, which seemed a miracle. They had been so long away from Lindisfarne that they had forgotten that it was cut off at high-tide. But they were soon back at Durham, and when William himself arrived there on his way back from Scotland, in doubt about the whereabouts and miraculous nature of St Cuthbert's body, they assured him that it was still in its shrine and still uncorrupt. But he wanted to see for himself and insisted on having the coffin opened. On the morning when this was to happen, he was taken with a violent fever, which was so plainly the effect of the saint's wrath at the intended sacrilege, that in a fright he immediately set off for York, and never drew rein until he was safely across the Tees. Sometime during his stay in Durham, he had made sure that the Norman presence there should not be challenged again, by ordering a great castle to be built on the site of an earlier Saxon fortification.

Norman influence was to be paramount. The last Saxon bishop was frightened out of his see and disgraced. Aethelwin knew what difficult terms he was on with the Conqueror, and thought it would be wise to get out of his way. He wanted to go to Cologne, but since he had no money of his own for the journey, he was forced to take what he needed from the community. After a winter in Scotland he was trying to make his way south, when he was captured at Ely and imprisoned at Abingdon by order of the King. He swore that he had taken nothing belonging to the Church, but as he was washing his hands a bracelet dropped out of his sleeve, and he was judged guilty. He died of starvation, some said because he refused to eat, others because no food was given him.[5]

In his place William appointed the first Norman bishop, Walcher of Lorraine, who had been a canon of Liége. Tall and handsome, with white hair and a fresh complexion, he was an imposing figure, and Queen Edith, the widow of Edward the Confessor, prophesied that he would become a martyr. His importance was greatly increased when the Conqueror made him Earl of Northumbria in place

4

of Waltheof, who was executed in 1076. During the ten years of his episcopate he began some building at Durham, intending to revive the strict Benedictine rule there, as was being done in other parts of England.

Three monks, hoping to revive the ancient glories of Northumbria, had already arrived from the south, carrying by turns as they journeyed the books and vestments that they needed. Walcher settled them in Bede's ruined monastery at Jarrow. As their numbers grew, some went to Melrose, others founded a house at St Mary's, York; eventually Walcher recalled them and gave them Wearmouth, the other half of Bede's monastery. Among them was a Lincolnshire man named Turgot, who had rebelled against William and had fled to Norway, before becoming a monk. Walcher was killed by a riotous mob in Gateshead, who were incensed by an atrocious murder done by his officer.

A few months later, in 1081, the King appointed another Norman to the see. The new bishop was abbot of St Vincent, but since in his younger days he had been a monk of St Carileph, he is generally known as William of St Carileph or St Calais. Carileph, with his strict monastic training, was outraged by what he found at Durham. The clergy attached to the White Church were neither monks nor canons regular, and neither their manner of worship nor their discipline was very satisfactory. Carileph determined to carry out his predecessor's intention of replacing them with men who would follow the strict Benedictine rule, but he went cautiously about it. Walcher's death warned him that the Saxons could be dangerous. Having got the support of the Pope, the King, and Archbishop Lanfranc, he provided for the members of the old community by placing them with the canons regular at Auckland, Norton, and Darlington; the prior wished to stay on, and become a Benedictine. The monks whom Walcher had placed at Jarrow and Wearmouth were brought to Durham, and their considerable endowments transferred to their new establishment. In later days it was claimed that Carileph gave his foundation wide lands and great privileges, but the documents which seem to support this claim have been proved forgeries which were no doubt manufactured to substantiate rights already exercised.[6] The reality seems to be that he gave them a small endowment, which he intended to increase later on, but he did not live to do so. No clear division was made between the property of the bishop, and the community, and this, later on, was one cause of continuing disputes between the two. The earldom of Northum-

5

bria, which Walcher held, passed on his death to Alberic, and then into the stronger hands of Robert de Mowbray, causing considerable friction between the temporal and spiritual powers in the region. At the king's suggestion Carileph bought Robert de Mowbray's rights, and so could exercise semi-regal authority. It is from this purchase that the Palatine jurisdiction, so long held by the bishop of Durham, is said to derive.[7]

# 3
# THE NORMAN CATHEDRAL

Carileph was a favourite minister of William Rufus, and spent much of his time at court. In the suspicion and intrigue, which abounded there, he involved himself in the rebellion of Odo of Bayeux, the King's uncle, and was forced to take refuge in Normandy. After three years there he managed to do the King a service, which put him into favour again, and he could come back to England. Whether it was during this time that he decided to build a new cathedral at Durham, or whether it had always been his intention to do so, it is impossible to say, but it was probably then that he finally made up his mind. The White Church was in its way a splendid building, and it was comparatively new. But the Norman stamp had to be placed on all the power centres in Church and State. Prestige was as important then as now. If the Saxons had built a fine church, the Normans would build a finer. 'The Durham Castle and Cathedral that we know, rose as the symbols of a new Latin civilization, superimposed on these wild Nordic lands by a foreign soldiery and clergy.'[8]

When Carileph came back to Durham, he brought with him books and sacred objects for the church which he intended to build. He first pulled down the White Church, and then, on 29 July 1093, he and Turgot, the Saxon rebel from Lincolnshire, who was now the prior of the new monastery, helped to dig the foundations for the building. On 11 August, the foundation stone itself was laid in the presence of Malcolm, king of Scotland. The noblest piece of Norman architecture on one of the finest sites in Europe had been begun. We do not know who the architect was, but possibly it was William of St Carileph himself; whoever he was, he is among the great builders of all time. The massive grandeur of the conception was equalled by the skill with which it was executed. As a feat of engineering alone, carried out as it was with the primitive means of that day, it was an amazing achievement. The work went quickly on. Carileph had been accumulating money for it for some time; there must have been a large quantity of cut stone from the White Church, which was usable, and plenty more could be obtained from quarries nearby. He probably completed the choir from the East End and the nave as far as the second bay; including the great arches, which would later on support the tower. As he built it, the East End had three apses, the centre one circular both inside and out, the others circular on the inside, and square outside. Not until a long time after did the East End take on its present shape.[9]

Carileph cannot have been much in Durham, for he was an active member of the King's court. Either from conviction, or perhaps because he had no wish to go on his travels again, he supported Rufus in his quarrel with Anselm over the rival claims of the Crown and the Church, but there was no lasting animosity between the two bishops. Anselm visited Carileph at Windsor in his last illness during Christmastide 1095 and gave him his blessing. On New Year's Day Carileph asked that he might receive the last rites from the Archbishop of York, the Bishop of Winchester, and the Bishop of Bath and Wells, and that they might hear his profession of faith. To them he commended the care of his monks, whom he 'dearly loved'. Afterwards, talking among themselves, the three bishops agreed that he ought to be buried at Durham in the new cathedral, because of the great care he had shown for the honour of St Cuthbert. The dying man overheard what they said, and protested that he was unworthy of being laid near the saint, and asked that his grave should be in the Chapter house; it was there that they buried him.

William Rufus kept the see vacant for three years and five months and then gave it to Rannulph Flambard, his chaplain and most powerful minister. Flambard was an energetic and picturesque ruffian, whose wickedness astounded the medieval chroniclers.[10] His origin is obscure. One story is that he started life in the service of the Bishop of London, and then moved to that of the King. Finding money was his main task; and, as one way of doing that, he suggested that church preferment should be kept vacant as long as possible, and the revenues go to the Crown. He managed to squeeze out all that Rufus asked for, and a good deal more. So long as the King was on his side he did not care whom he offended, but that made him enemies and nearly cost him his life. One day, somewhere along the banks of the Thames, he was met by an old retainer of his called

Gerold, with a message that the Bishop of London was dying, and wished to see him. They got into a boat, but instead of going in the right direction, it dropped downstream, and Rannulph was forced into a ship full of armed men. He was separated from his servants, but before that happened he managed to throw his own seal, and that of his secretary, overboard, to prevent his captors making use of them. The ship put to sea and it was arranged for two of the sailors to murder Rannulph and have his clothes for their trouble. But while they argued about who should have what, a storm blew up, which frightened everybody except Rannulph. By offering money to the crew, and some appeal to Gerold's fealty, he persuaded them not to kill him, but to set him ashore instead. Once on shore he entered London at the head of a great retinue of knights; and Gerold, knowing the man he had to deal with, wisely disappeared. A little while after Rannulph was made bishop of Durham.

William Rufus was killed while out hunting in the New Forest, by an arrow which came from no one knew where. His successor, Henry I, shut Rannulph up in the Tower of London for all his varied crimes, but he was not the man to give in tamely. He had a large flagon of wine brought in, with a rope inside. The wine was used to make the guards drunk, and the rope for the bishop's escape. But he was fat and he had forgotten to bring his gloves, though he had thought to bring his pastoral staff.[11] The rope was too short; it cut his hands badly, and the drop at the end shook him up a good deal; but friends were waiting with horses, and he got safely away to Normandy, accompanied by his mother, who was said to be a witch with one eye, in a separate ship. Rannulph could always find a niche for himself. At one time he and his mother were said to be mixed up with pirates. Duke Robert, Henry's brother, used him in the government of Normandy and he contrived to get some church preferment as well. When the brothers managed to patch up their quarrel, he was allowed to return to England again.

The work on Durham Cathedral had not stood still since William of St Carileph's death. The arrangement had been that the bishop should build the church, and the community the monastic buildings, but during the vacancy in the see they had gone on and completed the West Side of the transepts. Flambard took up the bishop's share, but only allotted to it the funds which came from 'altar and cemetery' so the work went on by fits and starts, as money was available. He finished the nave as high as the roof, leaving it no doubt boarded in; for the stone vaulting was ultimately put on while the monks were waiting for Flambard's successor. Like his predecessor he was a busy man outside the diocese and cannot often have been present himself.

## 4
## THE UNCORRUPT BODY TRANSLATED

But he was in Durham on 24 August 1104 when the cathedral was at last ready to receive the body of St Cuthbert. Since the destruction of the White Church, it had rested in a splendid shrine in the cloisters; now it was to be moved to a place behind the high altar. Later on the vacant place in the cloisters was filled with a finely carved and gilded image of St Cuthbert in his vestments as when he used to say Mass, with his mitre on his head, and a crosier in his hand 'marvellous to behold'.[12] A great many notables had come together for the final enshrinement of the sacred body and there was a good deal of discussion among them about whether, in fact, it was still there, and if so, whether it was still undecayed. It was 418 years since the saint's death, and while miracles were still being performed at his tomb, might that not be by the power of the sanctity which lingered there, though the body was gone? But nobody was willing to risk the sacrilege which would be involved in an examination.[13] St Cuthbert had not always been treated with so much awe. The sacrist, Elfrid Westoue, the man who stole Bede's bones, used to open the coffin whenever he felt like it, and wrap the body in such robes as he thought fit. He would also cut the saint's hair and nails, rounding the nails off very nicely with a pair of silver scissors that he had made. In the sight of all he would also hold a piece of the saint's hair in the flames, where it would glisten like gold, and then, when it was taken away, go back to its former colour. Now the days of such familiarity were over. But at last, with a great reluctance, it was decided to see what the coffin did indeed contain.[14]

Nine of the brethren, with Turgot the prior, were selected for the task. They prepared themselves with fasting and prayer, and on the night of 24 August 1104, with much trepidation they opened the tomb. Inside they found a large chest, covered with leather which had been nailed over it. This they must have carried into the church, as the actual examination took place in the choir. After much hesitation, they went on to explore further and found a second coffin inside, covered with three thicknesses of coarse linen. Recollecting that Bede had described such a coffin as containing the

9

saint's body when it was in Lindisfarne, they thought that they had discovered enough, and that it would be sacrilege to go further. But one of them, an Englishman called Leofwine—Dear Friend—a man of great sanctity, encouraged them to proceed. They stripped off the linen and examined the coffin, to see if there was any chink through which they could look inside without disturbing it any more, but they could not find one. So they opened it and found a second lid, which had an iron ring at each end to enable it to be lifted out. A copy of the Gospels lay on this, towards the head. They were approaching the crucial point in their search, and were more terrified than ever, but at the prior's order they lifted the lid. When they moved the linen cloth that lay beneath, an odour of the sweetest fragrance greeted them; and there, lying on its right side, whole, entire and uncorrupt, looking as if he was asleep, lay the body of St Cuthbert.

Awe-stricken they prostrated themselves and said the seven penitential psalms; then, taking courage, they examined the body still further. They saw that it had been placed on its side, in order to make room for a great many bones of other saints, among them those of the Venerable Bede in a linen bag. Under these there were some signs of decay, but none under the body of St Cuthbert. With him were the instruments for saying Mass: a small chalice and paten, the chalice being of purest gold made in the shape of a lion, with a hollowed out onyx stone on its back; a silver portable altar; and a linen cloth for covering the consecrated elements. In order to take out the relics of the other saints and put them in a place by themselves, they decided to move the body of St Cuthbert; but for a long time they were afraid to touch it. Leofwine again encouraged them, and two monks took it, one by the head and the other by the feet. When they tried to lift it they found that it sagged in the middle, as it would have done if it had been alive, so another monk supported it underneath, and between them they laid it reverently on the floor, which had been covered with carpets and cloths. When they had taken out the other bones, they put the body back, intending to return the next night to arrange it better.

Next morning they told the brethren of their marvellous experience and there was great rejoicing. During the day they made a false bottom for the coffin, because of the way in which the miscellaneous relics had stained the other one. When night came, they again moved the body, took out all the other bones except the head of St Oswald, for preservation in another part of the church, put in the new board and returned the body, wrapped in a new silk shroud, to its coffin, together with the instruments for the Mass, an ivory comb, and a pair of silver scissors, which they also found there. They must have kept the linen cloth for covering the sacred elements, for it was afterwards to play an important part in the fortunes of England. This done, they wrapped the coffin in a linen cloth soaked in wax and returned it to its place. The building was ready for the translation, except that the woodwork supporting the new apse was still in place, and it was doubtful if it could be taken down in time; but the night before the ceremony it collapsed, as it was thought by St Cuthbert's own intervention.

News of the examination which had been made spread among the guests, but it did not remove their earlier scepticism. Why had it been done in the dead of night? Why had only Durham monks been present? Though the community was hurt and angry that they were not believed, Turgot agreed to a suggestion of the Abbot of Séez that a further scrutiny should be made, and this time with independent witnesses. With a considerable number of people present the coffin was opened once more, and the Abbot of Séez, with one assistant, lifted up the body, moved the arms and legs and tweaked the ears, to prove their flexibility. All others were warned to stand back and not to touch even a thread of what was in the coffin. Now, apparently, everybody was convinced. But what was in fact the actual state of the body? If it was mummified, surprise at finding it undecayed and the reverential awe provoked by the sight would be enough to make those present see it with some exaggeration.

The ceremonies might now begin. The date was 29 August 1104. After a solemn Te Deum the great procession left the church. First went many relics of the saints, then a group of monks chanting hymns, then the coffin of St Cuthbert covered with Flambard's best cope, which was set down in the open for all to see. Flambard preached, and went on and on, dragging in all sorts of things which had no relation to what they were doing, until everybody was very bored. A lucky shower stopped him at last. The monks picked up St Cuthbert and scuttled with him into the church; it was taken as a miracle that the rich vestments in use were undamaged by the rain. Flambard had still another twenty-four years to live. An able, if ruthless administrator, he settled the bishoprick firmly under Norman rule. He did a good deal of building, including the bridge across the Wear at Framwellgate, which is still in use. He was a courtier, a lawyer, and something of a wit, and he was not without friends; but his scandalous life was an insult to the Church he served. Towards the end his health began to fail and he started to repent with a good deal of ostentation. He paid his debts and gave a great sum of money to the poor, which the King took back again as soon as he was out of the way. He died on 5 September 1128, leaving at least three sons and a number of relatives provided for in the Church.

His successor was Geoffrey Rufus who, like Flambard, was one of the King's ministers. The two great doors to the nave of the cathedral, one on the North Side, with the famous knocker, and the other on the South with its twelfth-century iron-work, were made in his time. The beauty of the stone and the skill of the workmanship make them outstanding features of a noble building. Almost as important to the life of the community as the church itself was the chapter house, where the monks assembled each day to settle their ordinary business. This was also the work of Geoffrey Rufus, and though largely rebuilt in the nineteenth century, can still be seen in its main features. The great stone chair at the East End was there for the bishop to preside in; the prior's seat was a simpler wooden one, placed by its side, while the monks sat on stone benches north and south.[15]

5

# USURPATION AND CHAOS

The bishoprick of Durham, so near to the border and so wealthy, was obviously a desirable acquisition for the Scots. In the breakdown of authority under King Stephen, it looked as if they might have a chance to take it. King David of Scotland had a chancellor called William Cumin, who was also a priest in the household of Geoffrey Rufus, and was with him during his last illness in Durham Castle at Easter time 1140.[16] It was an opportunity too good to be missed. Cumin put himself forward as the next bishop. The garrison of the castle declared for him, as did most of the barons of the Palatinate and the leading clergy, except for Roger the prior and the archdeacons of Durham and Northumberland. Leaving orders with his friends to conceal the Bishop's death until he got back, Cumin hurried off to Scotland to let King David know what he had done and, through him, obtain the support of Matilda, Stephen's rival for the throne of England. The Bishop died while Cumin was away, and the people in the castle disembowelled his body and salted it, so that it would keep until the secret of his death could come out. Cumin managed to hold on for three years, trying with ferocious cruelty to break down all opposition. Then letters came from Rome ordering the monks to elect a bishop in any place where it was safe for them to do so. They chose William of St Barbara, the dean of York, the place where they were meeting. The new Bishop came to take possession of his see, but Cumin's men met him, drove him into St Giles' church on the outskirts of Durham, and besieged him there. The monks barricaded themselves in the cathedral, but Cumin's men took it by storm; some of them forcing their way in at the windows and then opening the doors to let in the rest. Knights and archers chased the clergy through the building, driving them with drawn swords from the altars, until they had cleared the place and put in a garrison of their own. The shocked chronicler records how the cathedral then became a fortress, with soldiers quartered in every part, eating, sleeping, cooking, and cleaning their arms in the house of prayer. Cumin himself was raging through the bishoprick, until he realized that his cause was hopeless and made his submission. William of St Barbara spent the nine years of his episcopate repairing the terrible ravages of the war. The people had been harried to death, their houses and churches destroyed, and all semblance of law had disappeared. It is no wonder that he was looked back upon with great affection.

6

## THE MAGNIFICENT DU PUISET

William of St Barbara died in November 1152, and in February 1153 the Durham monks met to elect his successor. The times were desperate. Northumberland and Cumberland were in the hands of the Scots. The last Viking raid in English history was to devastate Yorkshire during that year. In quieter times they might have chosen either Laurence the prior or Wazo the archdeacon, for either of them would have been glad of the post, but now they needed a strong man, and preferably one with a good deal of influence. They chose Hugh du Puiset.[17] He was between twenty-five and thirty, which was below the canonical age for a bishop, the nephew and protégé of Henry of Blois, bishop of Winchester, who possibly recommended him. He already had three children by three different women; and though he was both archdeacon of Winchester, and treasurer of York, showed no aptitude for the religious life. But he came of a

13

thrusting line, and had proved himself an able administrator, and a tough opponent in the chaotic faction fights of the time. At York he had clashed with Archbishop Murdac, an austere man who bitterly resented his election and excommunicated the electors for proceeding without his authority, though Durham was never willing to allow the right of York to interfere. The monks appealed to Rome and sent their bishop elect with a deputation to the Pope; supported by the Archbishop of Canterbury, who had lifted the excommunication, and carrying a letter from the Bishop of Winchester. Murdac's representative urged against du Puiset his youth and irregular life. The Durham deputation replied that Joash had been king of Judah when only seven and David had been old in counsel though young in years. The Pope was convinced, and du Puiset's election was confirmed. He was consecrated in Rome on 20 December 1153.

Durham had got a bishop who would leave a broad, and deep, mark on both the bishoprick and the cathedral; to which he gave an aura of splendour, which was never lost throughout the Middle Ages. He saw himself less as a father in God than a great territorial lord, with all the restless self-aggrandizement of such a magnate. The Scots were near and dangerous neighbours, to be handled with care, and the Bishop's dealings with them brought his loyalty to the English Crown under suspicion. When Richard planned his crusade, du Puiset took a vow to go with him, raising large sums for the expedition and spending some of it on a silver throne and a lavishly equipped galley for the journey. But the King, who wanted the Bishop's money, more than his company, turned his mind from the project by selling him the earldom of Northumberland for life, and that of Sadberge to the bishoprick for ever, for £11,000. During the King's absence, he was made Regent of All England north of the Humber; but Longchamps, the chancellor of England, saw that he got very little good out of it. When Richard was safely home again, there was continual bickering between him and du Puiset about money, for the Bishop made no secret of Durham's riches. He was a noble builder. Darlington church, the hospital for lepers at Sherburn, and Elvet Bridge leading into the city of Durham were all his work, and more besides. Up to then, there had been no place of their own for women in the abbey, so du Puiset decided to build a Lady Chapel. Purbeck marble, which was coming into fashion now that William of Sens had used it at Canterbury, and stone for the pillars and bases were brought by sea to Newcastle and sent on by wagon

14

to Durham. He began to build at the East End of the church. His architect, Richard de Ingeniator or Richard the Engineer, was highly skilled and had done work both for the Bishop and the King which is among the finest of its period, but he was unable to cope with the difficulties of the site. The foundations slipped and the walls cracked. This was taken as a sign that St Cuthbert, who was said to dislike women, did not want them so near to him. The builders therefore moved to the West End and started afresh. Architecture had developed since the cathedral was built and du Puiset's chapel was in a new style transitional from Norman to Early English. In its first days it must have seemed even lighter and more graceful than it does now, for the arches were supported by only two shafts of Purbeck Marble, the other two of stone being added later. This chapel came to be called the Galilee, probably because the great Sunday procession, which symbolized Our Lord's return to Galilee, ended there.

All the life of the monastery was built up round the Seven Hours of Prayer, in which the whole Psalter was read through once a week. At Durham, Mattins was said at midnight, Lauds came near to daybreak, and Prime just after it was light. Terce or the Third Hour of the Day was halfway between sunrise and noon, Sext at Mid-day, Nones came in the afternoon, followed by Vespers between five and six and Compline just before bed-time. The different Masses for the community and for individuals were fitted in during the morning. The ordinary work and study of the monastery was carried on between the services, a great part of it in the cloisters. These, which in our day have become a symbol of quiet, were then the scene of a continuous and regulated activity. A medieval cathedral was really two churches; the smaller one, consisting of the high altar, and the choir, was the normal place for the devotions of the religious community; this was entered through a doorway in the elaborate stone screen dividing it from the nave which, with its various altars, was open to all except women.

Monastic life was disciplined and ordered, but the many festivals offered opportunities for variety and splendour. The vestments and ornaments of the church were elaborate and costly; for the art and wealth of the time were lavished on their creation. Du Puiset at the altar, in his red velvet chasuble, 'nobly embroidered in gold and bezants, and studded with great pearls and precious stones', or if he wore his black one, 'emblazoned with a bizarre assortment of jewels, golden stars, and griffins', must have been a sight to see. A great complex of buildings grew up to serve the various needs of the community, until they filled almost the entire Peninsula to the south of the cathedral. Their general outline can still be seen in the grouping of the houses which have sprung up on their foundations. The monastery which du Puiset knew was, no doubt, less elaborate than it became in later days, but the signatures on documents still extant show that it had all the officials of a fully developed Benedictine community. In addition to those belonging to the prior's household, there was a sub-prior and two, or sometimes more, sacrists, who were responsible for everything to do with the services of the church. The feretrar had the care of the shrines, and the chancellor charge of the legal business. Hospitality was one of the duties of the monastery, and this was supervised by the hostillar; there was also a clerk of the cellar and a cook. The infirmary for sick monks, the almonry where gifts were made to the poor, and the hostelry or guest house, 'were all well established with separate endowments, and considerable control of their own affairs' by the end of du Puiset's episcopate.[18]

The Durham abbey had become a great house of learning. Canon law was closely studied, and there was a better knowledge of classical literature at Durham than in most other places. Theology was much in evidence, with a good deal of attention being paid to biblical exegesis. The Bishop himself had two great Bibles and a number of commentaries on the Scriptures, which in their writing, binding, and illumination, were among the most splendid examples of their art. The work of the Durham scribes was 'a last glorious reflection of Northumbrian traditions'. The Durham monastery 'was then at the height of its literary and intellectual distinction, magnificently housed in one of the most superb churches of western Christendom, and endowed with the enormous prestige of the name of Cuthbert, and the wealth of a patrimony, containing the best part of the one-time kingdom of Northumbria'.[19] Outlying priory churches were growing into cells of the mother house with monks coming and going between them at the discretion of the prior. The wealth and importance of Durham overshadowed every other monastic institution in the bishoprick.

Over all this towered the imperious and splendid du Puiset, impatient of anyone who tried to curtail his income or resist his will. He died in 1195 through over-eating, it was said, as he was on his way to London to see the King. The monks had maintained a resolute struggle against him in the effort to retain their revenue

16

and their privileges. Much of what they wanted they obtained, as the Bishop lay on his death-bed in that fit of repentance which generally overtook medieval despots, when they neared their end. But they had to fight for it all over again, and with even greater bitterness, under du Puiset's two successors. The first was Philip of Poitou, who excommunicated the Prior, and in the effort to subdue the monks tried to cut off their food and water and destroyed their fish ponds. There was even a fight at the high altar, when the Bishop's officers tried to prevent Mass being said, by taking away the altar linen, and the monks struggled with them for it. The dispute was patched up for a time, but broke out again under Bishop Marsh, King John's chancellor, who succeeded to the see after a nine-years vacancy and swore that the Durham monks should never have peace as long as he lived. The monks supported their case by the charters, which were supposedly granted by William of St Carileph but are undoubtedly forgeries. Both sides spent large sums of money in their cause. The Prior appealed to Rome, the Bishop went to London, to get help from the King, but died at Peterborough as he was on the way to see him. Similar disputes, though not always as virulent, were going on all over England, as the monasteries tried to assert their independence of the Bishop and he, in his turn, to claim what he believed to be his rights.

7

## THE CHAPEL OF THE NINE ALTARS

There is no record of any addition to the cathedral, after the building of the Galilee, until Bishop le Poor planned the chapel of the Nine Altars, though it was not actually begun until 1242, five years after his death, when Thomas Melsonby was prior. William of St Carileph's East End had been showing signs of collapse for some time and rebuilding was urgently needed. To raise money for this different bishops offered indulgences, which recited the great fame and virtues, of St Cuthbert and enjoined the faithful to give liberally for the renovation of his shrine. Those who did so would receive thirty days remission of penance. The architect for the new building was Richard of Farnham, though Elias of Dereham, the greatest architect of his day, was in Durham in 1229 and may have supplied the inspiration, for the soaring delicate beauty of the work reflects what he had already achieved at Salisbury cathedral, which Bishop le Poor had begun to build when he was in that see.[20]

Prior Melsonby, who carried the project through, very nearly missed being confirmed in his office. It was objected to him that he had allowed a medieval Blondin to try to walk on a tight-rope, stretched between two towers of the cathedral, with disastrous results, for the poor man had fallen and killed himself.[21] His attempt was a little out of the ordinary run of entertainment no doubt, but the feretrar's accounts, which show how money collected at the shrine was spent, record a number of payments to players and singers, so the community was not without occasional diversions. Since there were many priests in the monastery needing to say Mass, the new chapel had nine altars for their use. Projecting into it and on a level with the high altar in the main church was St Cuthbert's shrine; this was the heart of the cathedral and the magnet for a stream of pilgrims from all over England, whose offerings added to its already great riches. But not all visitors were generous. When Henry III called in 1255, chronically in debt on account of his wife's relatives and his own ambitious building projects, he learned that a great quantity of treasure, belonging to the bishop of Durham and the bishop of Ely, as well as other clergy, had been sent for safe-keeping to the shrine. He had the locks and seals broken open, and took it for his own use, explaining that he was merely borrowing it for a time, but he paid none of it back.

The prior of Durham was a very great man. He presided at all chapter meetings and was the source of all authority in the monastery. His rank was equal to that of the great border lords, and he outshone them in splendour. When he visited the outlying houses of the order, he went with a train of attendants and took with him his own furniture and the means of saying Mass in a splendid wagon drawn by horses in red harness. If he retired from office, he was given a household suited to his rank, and was allowed apartments and an income, which meant little diminution of his earlier state.

In 1260 the bishoprick went to Robert Stichill a Durham monk, who was the illegitimate son of a priest. As a novice, for some fault, he had been made to sit on a stool in the middle of the choir and in a temper had kicked it out into the nave. Then he decided to run away, but as he was passing a crucifix in the church, he heard a voice calling him back. He stayed, and became so much loved that, unknown to him, a dispensation was obtained from Rome to allow him to become a bishop, in spite of his parentage. He justified his appointment and, among other acts of charity, founded the hospital at Greatham.[22]

Determined as the Durham monks were to resist the encroachments of their own bishop, they were even more resolute against those of the archbishop of York. In 1280, the dispute between them was particularly fierce. The Archbishop attempted to present a candidate of his own to a Yorkshire church which belonged to the Durham community, and was strongly resisted. He then threatened to hold an official visitation of the Durham monks and they, supported by their bishop, defied him. But in 1283 the bishop, Robert of Holy Island, died. He had been a good, humble, man; simple in his habits, generous to the abbey, and very devoted to his mother, to whom he gave everything he could think of to make her happy. When he asked her if she was satisfied, she said that she was not. Everybody was so obedient and respectful to her that she never had a chance to ease her mind with a burst of bad-temper. Robert's death gave the Archbishop another chance to assert himself by claiming the care of the see during the vacancy. He arrived at Durham to carry out the visitation that he had threatened. As the monks refused to let him into the abbey, he withdrew to the church of St Nicholas in the city and preached a strong sermon, threatening to excommunicate the prior and the whole community. However, the young men of Durham rallied to the prior's defence, and chased the Archbishop out of the place, wounding his horse and barely letting him escape with his life. Disputes with the archbishop of York crop up again and again throughout the succeeding centuries, as the archbishop continually tried to assert what he thought were his metropolitan rights, and both the bishop, and the cathedral, as regularly repulsed him.

## 8
# THE MOST VALIANT CLERK
# IN CHRISTENDOM

Antony Bek, Robert of Holy Island's successor, was consecrated at York during the Christmas-time 1283 in the presence of the King and a great company of nobles.[23] The next day, the Archbishop, who had by no means forgotten the way in which he had been treated by the Durham monks, demanded that the new Bishop should excommunicate both them and their Prior. But he was talking to the wrong man. Bek had no intention at all of being subservient to his metropolitan. 'Yesterday,' he said, 'I was consecrated their bishop, and shall I excommunicate them today?' Bek came of a Lincolnshire family which already had connections with Durham. His grandfather and father had been vassals of the bishop, and his father had given the community there the advowsons of three parishes in return for their prayers for him and his successors. Antony's great abilities had been recognized very early. In 1270 he had been sent by Henry III to accompany Prince Edward on a crusade and had been nominated as one of those who were to administer England, if there was a vacancy in the Crown. He held five benefices in the diocese of Canterbury, and in 1279 was made archdeacon of Durham. His arrival as bishop was viewed by the monks with some apprehension, but they comforted themselves with the thought that at least he would stand up to the Archbishop of York. He was not enthroned until 1285, and showed at once that he was going to have his own way everywhere. The prior claimed the right to enthrone him, which Bek refused to allow. Instead, he had the ceremony performed by his brother, the bishop of St David's.

That was on 24 December 1285. On the 27th, he called a meeting of the monks, from which he excluded the prior, Richard Claxton, and the sub-prior, Richard Hoton. Claxton was eased out of his office on the ground that he wished to resign, though he did not. Hoton was passed over and Hugh Darlington was brought back again. He had filled the post with distinction in his day. In a difficult time he had managed to preserve, and even increase, the abbey's possessions. The poor danced before him when he made his progress from one of the community's houses to another, knowing that, wherever he was, there would be unstinted hospitality for them. So that he might scatter handfuls of largess from his chariot as he went along, he had a special coin minted, called a mite, which had the value of one fifth of an old penny, by no means a contemptible sum in those days. As he was then he was summed up as 'a man of approved wisdom and magnificent mind'.[24] But in 1272, after fourteen years as prior, he asked to be relieved of his post owing to increasing infirmity. Brought back again, he was old, stubborn, unwilling to listen to advice, and by no means capable of dealing with a man like Bek.

Hoton became, and remained, the Bishop's implacable opponent. In March 1289, when Darlington finally retired, he was elected prior; from then on he stood out as the guardian of his own rights and of the monastery's privileges and resources. He was a man of learning, with a graceful person and persuasive eloquence. Sometimes the pope and the king were on one side in the dispute, sometimes on the other.

Both sides had money to spend, and used it freely. When Hoton died at Poitiers on 9 January 1308, he was on his way back from Rome, where he had appealed against the Bishop's attempt to prevent him administering the affairs of the monastery, and had won his case. A man who could resist Antony Bek so long, and so successfully, must have had more than ordinary courage and ability.[25]

While all this wrangle was going on, Bek's public career was one of continuous splendour. He was the great minister of a great king and his chief adviser on Scottish affairs. In 1290 he helped to arrange the marriage of Prince Edward with Margaret of Scotland, and was an important influence in all the negotiations with Balliol. He took part in Edward's expedition against the Scots in 1296, followed by twenty-six standard bearers and a great retinue; though his Durham vassals objected, that their only obligation was to defend the patrimoney of St Cuthbert and not to engage in foreign wars. He negotiated loans for Edward I, served him as a diplomat at the papal court and at the courts of France, Germany, Norway, Flanders, and Aragon, and was the intimate friend of the King; though that did not prevent strong disagreement between them from time to time. In 1307 Edward II exalted him still further, by making him King of Man, and he also held the empty dignity of Patriarch of Jerusalem. His pride and magnificence became legendary, supported as they were by the wealth of Durham and his own family estates; but though he had vast riches, he seemed to be contemptuous of them, except as a means of dazzling those lesser people whom they impress. He heard once that a London merchant had a piece of cloth, which he claimed was too expensive even for the bishop of Durham. He sent for the man, bought his stuff, and had it cut up into horse-cloths in his presence.

Though he was fond of hawks and horses and the usual pastimes of a medieval baron, there was a strain of asceticism in him. He never had more than one sleep at night, getting up as soon as he woke, whatever the time might be. His generosity was lavish, and no one ever challenged his complete sexual purity. It was for these qualities, no doubt, that after his death in 1310, the Durham monks claimed that he was a saint, in spite of all that they had suffered from him. However that might be, Bek had undoubtedly been among the most outstanding men of his time. In the bishoprick he had consolidated, and increased, all the semi-regal powers which his predecessors had claimed, and asserted the complete independence of his see from the archbishop of York. He was in his day what a poet of the time called him, 'the most valiant clerk in Christendom'. Thinking perhaps that one great man at a time was enough, the chapter elected as his successor Richard Kellaw, a peaceable man and a scholar, who belonged to their own body and gave back to them all that Bek had taken away.

## 9
# THE NEVILLES AND THE RABY BUCK

In the continual battle against their powerful neighbours, the monks had not only to contend with the encroachments of the bishop and the archbishop, but also those of the great border lords. Notable among them was the family of Neville of Raby Castle. They held some part of their lands from the abbey at a yearly rent of £4, and a buck to be given to the monastery on 4 September, the feast of St Cuthbert. In 1290, Ralph, the third Lord Neville, claimed that when he came to present the buck, he and his retinue, and as many friends as he cared to bring, were to be entertained by the prior; perhaps he thought that if the whole thing were to become too burdensome, the presentation of the buck would be allowed to lapse. He also wanted to be waited on by his own servants rather than those of the abbey.[26] He arrived with a horde of people, but when his men tried to carry the buck into the kitchen, the prior, Hugh Darlington, refused to receive it. The argument grew fierce, Neville's men assaulted the monks, who seem to have moved into the church, where they defended themselves with the best weapons that they had at hand, namely the big wax candles which stood by the altar, and drove away the soldiers. The inevitable legal squabble followed. John Balliol of Barnard Castle, one of the local magnates, when appealed to, refused to support the Nevilles, saying that he had never heard of any such privilege. Sir William Brompton, the Bishop's Chief Justice, also condemned it, recollecting that, as a young man who delighted much in everything to do with the chase, he had been with the Lord Neville of the day at the presentation of the buck and had said to his companions, when the gift was made, 'Come, let us go into the abbey, and wind our horns,' but he never remembered any feasting, and the Prior claimed there had never been anything more than a breakfast.

The dispute died down, but it was started again by the fourth Lord Neville, also called Ralph. He insisted on being entertained for the whole day and for breakfast the day after. This was worse than ever and, of course, the prior objected strongly. Ralph replied that he would accept the judgement of his neighbours. The prior, who knew well enough that few of the local gentry dared displease a Neville and that the family had a good deal of influence at court, agreed that for one time only it should be as Lord Neville demanded; but that this condition should be put into writing to prevent a precedent being established. Ralph, having won his point, decided to be moderate. He came with only few friends, and went away at night, but left a servant to stay till morning, just to keep his claim alive.

There were other traditions too, that the monks were anxious to guard. One of them was that St Cuthbert had a strong dislike to women, and that none of them should approach his shrine nearer than the bar of Frosterly marble, let into the floor at the West End. One or two, who had disguised themselves and got in somehow, had suffered all sorts of pains and penalties in their persons from the angry saint. This prohibition applied even to the greatest. When, at Easter 1333, Queen Philippa came to join her husband Edward III at Durham and all unaware of the mistake she was making, rode boldly into the monastery, dined, and went to bed there, one of the monks was bold enough to tell the king how much St Cuthbert objected to such a proceeding. The poor lady was turned out of her bed and, in order to avoid going through the church, was sent round the outside of the abbey precincts to sleep at the castle.

Although their income must have suffered a good deal from the unrest in Scotland and on the border, the community under Prior Fossor, who was elected in March 1342, still managed to spend a good deal. The huge complex of buildings demanded continual repair, and an energetic prior was always anxious to add something new. John Lewyn, the principal mason to the abbey and the Palatinate in the latter part of the fourteenth century, designed for him the great kitchen with its vault of intersecting ribs which are a delight to the eye and a perfect support for the lantern. 'The resemblance of this to examples in Persia and Spain afford an unusual problem in the diffusion of style'.[27] It was in use as the kitchen of the deanery until 1940. Prior Fossor also rebuilt the smithy, slaughterhouse, brewhouse and barns, and other ancillary buildings. In the cathedral where the Norman windows gave too little light, and also, perhaps, offered insufficient opportunity for the wealth of stained glass he wished to install, he put in the great West Window and an equally splendid one in the South Transept.

There was no stint in the monks' hospitality. Though their ordinary fare was simple enough, a pound loaf of bread, two measures of ale, two portions of pulse or beans, and two of flesh or fish each day; when they kept open house on feast days, it was all lavishly done. The cellarer's list of provisions bought at Whitsuntide 1347, with the prices paid, makes interesting reading. There were:

'600 salt herrings, 3s; 400 white herrings, 2s 2d; 30 salted salmon, 7s 6d, 12 fresh salmon, 5s 6d; 14 ling, 55 kelengs [cod]; 4 turbot, 23s 1d; two horse loads of white fish, and a congr (conger eel?), 5s 10d; plaice, sparlings, and eels, and fresh-water fish, 2s 9d; 9 carcases of oxen salted, so bought, 36s; 1 carcase and a quarter fresh, 6s 11¾d; a quarter of an ox fresh, bought in the town, 3s 6d; 7 carcases and a half of swine in salt, 22s 2d; 6 carcases fresh, 12s 9d; 14 calves, 28s 4d; 3 kids and 26 sucking porkers, 9s 7d; 71 geese with their feed, 11s 10d; 14 capons, 59 chickens and 5 dozen pigeons, 10s 3d; 5 stones of hog's lard, 4s 2d; 4 stones of cheese, butter and milk, 6s 6d; a pottle of vinegar, and a pottle of honey, 6d; 14 pounds of figs and raisins, 13 pounds of almonds, and 8 pounds of rice, 3s 7d; pepper, saffron, cinnamon, and other spices, 2s 6d; 1300 eggs, 15s 5d; Sum total, £11 4s.'

Similar quantities were bought for the great feast days over a long series of years.[28]

Prior Fossor lived to be very old. When he was 90, he had a sort of litter made, so that he could be carried round, and still supervise the work that he loved. It was no doubt because of his long and distinguished service to the community that when he died in November 1374, they buried him in the abbey church itself, the first prior to lie there, rather than in the cloister garth with all his predecessors.

Great things happened in Prior Fossor's time. In 1346 Edward III was in France, and the Scots, egged on by the French, invaded England. King David crossed the border, plundering and laying waste in the usual way of medieval war. He reached the prior's summer residence at Beaurepaire (the present Bear Park) a few miles from the city. The border lords, Neville and Percy, were encamped at Bishop Auckland. In this crisis St Cuthbert appeared in a vision to Prior Fossor, telling him to take the Holy Corporax, the linen cloth for covering the Blessed Sacrament which had been found in the saint's coffin, one of the holiest relics which the church possessed, put it on a spear and carry it to the army. There on a hillock near the Red Hills, where the fight took place, the prior and his attendants knelt round it and prayed, while the battle raged.[29] The Scots had an equally famous talisman to rely upon, the Black Rood of Scotland, which was a silver crucifix with St John on one side and St Mary on the other. It was so ancient that it 'looked as if it had been smoked all over'. The Abbey of Holy Rood at Edinburgh had been built as its shrine. The two armies met on 17 October, and the Scots were crushed. The monks, watching the battle from the tower of their church, burst into the Te Deum as they saw the victory. The English army poured down to the abbey to return thanks, and Ralph, the fourth Lord Neville (he who had argued the second time about the buck) gave his own banner and that of the King of Scotland, now a prisoner, to St Cuthbert's shrine. The Black Rood itself was set up at the end of the South Aisle, near St Cuthbert's shrine, on a background of red woodwork, decorated with leaden stars gilded over.[30] The Corporax was mounted on red velvet, a yard wide, and made into a banner, which was much sought after for its power in every kind of crisis. Its last appearance was in 1513, at the Battle of Flodden, when it led the men of the bishoprick into the fight, under Sir William Bulmer. The Earl of Surrey, the English commander, had made a special journey to Durham to ask for its presence.[31]

In spite of occasional disagreements, the Neville family were great benefactors of Durham Abbey. In 1355 the same Ralph Neville presented a complete set of vestments for High Mass, of ruby-coloured velvet, richly embroidered with silk and gold, and set with large pearls, and images of saints in tabernacles; together with a cope, and two altar cloths, which the bishop of Durham, Bishop de Bury, had pledged with him for a hundred pounds of silver. The Bishop had intended them for a gift to the abbey, but had been forced to raise money on them instead. Ralph, the fourth Baron Neville of Raby, was buried in 1367, at the East End of the nave, before the Jesus altar, with all the pomp of a great lord. Since Bishop Hatfield was away from home, and Prior Fossor was 83 and very infirm, the ceremonies were carried out by the Abbot of St Mary's, York. For the first time a corpse was brought in through the great North Door, when Ralph Neville was carried on the shoulders of his knights. Even when Antony Bek was buried this had not been allowed, but a way had been broken through the East Wall of the Nine Altars to admit the coffin. For the splendour of the funeral the Neville family presented the sacrist with 950 pounds of wax for candles, and 60 torches. Eight horses were given, four for war, and four for peace; and with the horses went four men-at-arms with all their accoutrements. There were also three pieces of cloth-of-gold, dyed with indigo and interwoven with flowers. The new baron, John Neville, redeemed the four best horses for 100 marks, and when twelve of the torches and one of the pieces of cloth-of-gold was returned to him, as a superabundance of generosity, he sent 100 marks more. The two pieces of cloth-of-gold, which were kept, were made into vestments; and Lady Alice, Ralph's widow, gave the sacrist 120 pounds of silver for the repair of the church.[32]

There seemed to be no end to the generosity of the Nevilles. In 1372 John, Lord Neville, presented a new pedestal for St Cuthbert's shrine, of marble and alabaster; and contributed 500 marks towards the cost of a new screen, to stand between the high altar and the shrine. It came from the London workshop of Henry Yevele, the greatest architect of his time. His biographer claims that it was 'almost certainly designed by him and if so it is his masterpiece in the realm of pure art and ornament'.[33] Made of Caen stone, it was carved in sections, which were packed in barrels and sent by sea to Newcastle. Seven masons, took nearly a year to erect it; in addition to their maintenance, the monastery found another 200 marks to make up the cost. It still stands, fascinating in its slender beauty, and decorated with small delicate carvings; but it must have been even more splendid in its original state, with the niches, which are now empty, filled with 107 alabaster figures.

When Lady Alice Neville died and was buried with her husband before the Jesus altar, the gifts were again of a magnificence worthy of her house. The monastery had fifty pounds of wax, and each monk twenty shillings. The sacrist, who would be responsible for the funeral arrangements, had 300 pounds of wax and fifty torches. Her body was covered with three pieces of cloth-of-gold, one was of a ruby colour, interwoven with flowers. Another was black, patterned with branches, each bearing a white rose, and with leaves and beasts. These were made into copes. Two other pieces of ruby coloured stuff were also made into vestments. She had previously given the prior a black silk bed, embroidered with her arms, with its curtains, pillows, and blankets. Another gift was a set of vestments to be used on the anniversary of her death and that of her husband, which were embroidered with her arms and those of her father, Lord Audley. They must have stood out, even among the already riotous splendour of that great church. In 1416 the two bodies were removed from before the Jesus altar to a new chantry, which the Nevilles had been allowed to make on the South Side of the nave. Never before had such a thing been done in a place so wholly dedicated to St Cuthbert, but the services of the Nevilles to the abbey had been outstanding. There a priest, with a salary of £10 a year, said Mass each day for their souls. The effigies of Alice and her husband, mutilated by the Scots in 1640 and covered with the graffiti of centuries, still lie side by side in what was once their chantry. To the west of them lie the still more battered effigies of John, Lord Neville, and Matilda his wife.

In 1370 the shrine of the Venerable Bede was moved into the Galilee and placed on a pedestal of blue marble with a carved wooden canopy over it. On Ascension Day, Whitsunday, and Trinity Sunday, the shrine was taken, with the abbey's other relics, in procession out of the North Door of the church, round the outside of the chapel of the Nine Altars, and into the abbey again through the main gateway. Every monk had on a rich cope, the prior wearing one of cloth of fine gold, which was so heavy that he was compelled to have attendants on each side to ease its weight.

Fossor had become prior when Richard de Bury, who wrote *Philobiblion*, a famous work on book collecting and preservation, was bishop; but the greater part of his time in office was in the long episcopate of Thomas Hatfield. He was in the tradition of royal servants whom the King rewarded by the gift of a princely see. Occupied though he was, he still gave a good deal of attention to the affairs of his diocese and its abbey. He completed Durham College at Oxford, where promising young men were sent from Durham to complete their studies and enrich the life of the community on their return. At the Reformation its monastic connection brought it into disfavour and it was bought by Sir Thomas Pope, who refounded it as Trinity College. Being much in London he built Durham House in the Strand, which served the bishops of Durham as a residence until the Commonwealth. Hatfield was a good administrator, a man of great kindness and generosity, but his most lasting memorial is his tomb in the cathedral on the South Side of the choir. He built it, with the episcopal throne above it, in his lifetime, and his effigy in alabaster, comparatively undamaged by all the changes since, still lies where he wished it to be. Whoever the designer was—it could have been John Lewyn the architect of the Prior's Kitchen—he had in mind the Neville Screen which was going up close by.[34]

# 10

# YEARS OF GROWTH AND SPLENDOUR

The wealth and magnificence of the Durham monastic community is indicated by the Pope's reply to their request in 1372, that they might be allowed to appropriate the church of Hemmingburgh in Yorkshire. He had been informed, he wrote, that their body consisted of 150 persons, with four dependent abbeys and thirteen parishes, and the right of presentation to many more. When they rode abroad, he was told, they were each attended by three or four horsemen, and that the money they spent on food and clothing was far beyond what was seemly in a religious order. He could not grant their request. Somebody, not over friendly, may have been exaggerating a little, for the number of persons mentioned must have included dependents of many kinds; but on their own showing they were wealthy. Ten years later, they obtained for their prior the right of wearing the mitre, ring, and sandals, with the pastoral staff, which were pontifical insignia, on the ground that they had an income of 5000 marks and that other houses which had less had obtained that privilege.[35]

The cloisters, which were as essential to the life of the community as the church itself, were rebuilt by Bishop Skirlaw, who in his early days had been one of the Durham monks and had afterwards taken his LL.D at their college in Oxford. The work was not completed much before 1418, when Skirlaw had been dead twelve years, so it must have gone on slowly, though he left money for its completion.[36] By then Thomas Langley was bishop. The dormitory, begun at a later date than the cloisters, was finished by 1404, and was entirely within Skirlaw's time. Contracts for the work still exist in the cathedral archives. The first was made with John Middleton on 21 September 1398. He was to retain the old vault intact and build the walls on the pattern of the tower in Brancepeth Castle called 'Constabiltour'. There were to be nine windows, one for every two beds, so that the monks might have light for their studies. Everything needed, except for the wood and stone, which the prior, John Hemmingburgh, was to provide from somewhere within three miles of Durham, was to be found by Middleton. The work was to be finished in three years, and during that time he was to have, each year, a garment similar to that worn by the prior's esquires, and meat and drink for himself and his boy. He was to be paid £40 when he began, and thereafter, for every six and a half ells square which he finished, he was to receive ten marks of silver, and another £40 at the completion of every six roods, until the work was done. But Middleton failed to complete his contract, and another was made with Peter Dryng, on much the same terms, except that the food was specified as every day a white loaf, a flagon of beer, and a dish of meat from the kitchen, similar to that which the prior's esquires received.[37]

Thomas Langley, who became bishop in 1406 and cardinal in 1411, ranks with du Puiset and Bek as one of the three outstanding princes in the medieval history of Durham. Like them he served the king in high office and with much distinction, but we know less of his personal character than we do of theirs. However, glimpses of him can be seen in his official documents, which show him as a compassionate man, patient and skilful in his dealing with people, as fond of splendour as his two compeers, but unlike them, on good terms with the priors who ruled the monastery in his day. The money which Skirlaw had provided for the cloisters proved insufficient, and Langley gave another £240 for their completion. He put a window into the South Side of the church looking into the cloisters, and another in the Nine Altars. His most important building work, however, was carried on in the Galilee between 1428 and 1435. He put on a new roof, reinforced the crumbling structure, which was slipping into the river with massive buttresses, and added two stone pillars to each of the two slender marble shafts which supported the arches.[38]

Perhaps this renovation was carried out because in 1414 he had begun to prepare himself a chantry tomb in the Galilee, siting it before the great West Door of the cathedral, which he blocked up by doing so; and replacing that entrance by one on the South, and another on the North, which are still in use. Attached to the chantry was a school where two chaplains taught grammar and song to poor children free of charge; this was the small beginning from which the present public school has grown. The same care for the needs of the handicapped, which made him allow the poor people in du Puiset's reconstituted hospital of Sherburn to say their office in bed if they were sick or had grown feeble, made him obtain papal sanction for a font in the Galilee at which the children of excommunicated persons might be baptized. In the early years of the sixteenth century, and probably from Langley's time, there was 'a fair iron pulpit' with an iron handrail, standing facing Langley's tomb, and from it, one of the monks preached a sermon every Sunday and holy-day, at one o'clock in the afternoon. The bishop's consistory court was also in the Galilee, and the coming and going of litigants must have added considerably to the bustle of the place, which was decorated with brightly coloured crucifixion scenes above the spandrels and an ancient painting of St Cuthbert and King Oswald at the North End of the East Wall.

On 23 July 1408 Langley made an official visitation of the monastery. The prior stated that he had called in all the members of the community from the outlying cells, except those needed for carrying on the services there, and he gave a total of fifty-seven members. Revenues, though still great, were not what they had been. The northern estates, which in 1293 produced £1000 a year, yielded only £400 in 1430.[39] Loss of their lands in Scotland, and the continual raiding which went on across the border, together with the conversion of arable land to pasture, meant a drop in rents, which by 1436 had fallen to £353 a year. They still had profitable lands in Yorkshire, and there was income from spiritual sources of one kind and another, so they were still rich.

There seems to have been no major scandal among them, though, as was inevitable in such a body, there were black sheep from time to time. In 1407 Adam Durham who had run away with another monk named John Fishwick, and now roamed abroad as a layman, was ordered to be arrested and brought back. In the same year Thomas Esh quarrelled with Richard Stockton and wounded him with a knife. He was ordered to go to Rome for absolution, but he met the papal nuncio in London and obtained it from him, on the ground that he was too old and feeble to travel. One monk killed another, and one confessed to murder and was imprisoned.[40] These names, and many others, indicate that most of them came from places in the bishoprick. The great local family of Claxton provided a distinguished prior and some other members of the community. In spite of the misdemeanours of a few, when Bishop Neville visited the monastery in 1442, he could report that the morals of Durham and its cells were above reproach. But monasticism was losing its fervour. Monks were increasingly less active as social and religious pioneers and were becoming men who sought an ordinary, and sometimes self-indulgent, life away from the rough and tumble of the world. The Rule of St Benedict enjoined community of goods, yet by this time they had property of their own, for individuals among them contributed to the cost of work on their solar and washing arrangements.

In the thirty years of his rule Prior Wessington spent £6123 8s 7d on repairs to the abbey and its property. Some was needed for the central tower, the wooden spire of which was struck by lightning on 26 May 1429 and caught fire at one o'clock in the morning. By seven o'clock, when it was noticed, it was burning fiercely, and went on till midday. Wessington wrote off a full account at once to the bishop, to prevent him being worried by rumours. He is specially thankful, he says, that none of the ten or twelve men who worked among the flames and the molten lead, were injured. Patching up the damage cost £233 6s 8d, but twenty-six years later a complete re-building was needed, which was not finished, owing to shortage of funds, until about 1490. Thomas Barton would seem to have de-signed the lower stages with the lantern, which rises in austere beauty above the Norman arches of the crossing, but the upper part was completed by the second John Bell.

Pinched for money though they may have been at this time, they managed to provide well for Wessington when he retired. He was given a special apartment in the monastery with a monk, a gentle-man-in-waiting, a clerk, a valet, and a page to attend him, together with food and clothing for them all. He was also to have the income from certain churches and the best apartment in any daughter house he cared to visit. Numbers were growing during the first half of the fifteenth century. At Langley's election in 1406 fifty-seven monks were present. The same number attended his visitation in 1408. By 1416 there were sixty-nine, and when Bishop Neville was elected, in 1437, there were seventy-three. No doubt they put themselves out a good deal when the gentle King Henry VI visited Durham in 1448 and spent a few days in the castle, but they obviously impressed him. On Michaelmas Day, which fell on a Sunday, he attended the services in the abbey, and wrote, a fortnight later, that 'the church of the Province of York, and the Diocese of Durham, be as noble in doing of Divine Service, in multitude of ministers, and in sumptuous and glorious buildings, as any in our realm'.[41] Later on, when he was beset by his enemies, the Durham monks lent large sums of money to him and his supporters, many of whom were from the great local families. When Edward IV was in Durham in 1461, they tried to recover some of it, but without success.

By the end of the century, when Thomas Castell was elected prior, the community had fallen in numbers again; the list of members contained only forty-two names, though it may not have been com-plete. Castell continued the tradition of energetic priors. He added considerably to the landed property of the monastery and put in the great clock, which still stands in the South Transept of the cathedral. As the eastern gateway had fallen into a good deal of disrepair, he rebuilt it and the porter's lodge beside it, much as they stand today; with a chapel in honour of St Helen above the gate, which had two priests living in an apartment near-by, to say Mass twice a day for the laity. His personal tastes are shown by the fact that the bishop made him his game-warden, with the right to take deer from the episcopal forests as and when he pleased. He was present in 1503 at the North Door of the cathedral, with the bishop and all the monks richly vested, to receive the Princess Margaret who was on her way North to marry James IV of Scotland. As she passed through the city with 'the officers of arms, sergeants of arms, trumpets, and minstrels' going before her, every inch in the streets and every window was packed with people to see her go. In the abbey the Earl of Surrey presented her offering; she was given 'precious relics' to kiss, and so passed on into history to be the ancestress of the Stuart kings who ruled Great Britain with changing fortunes for nearly a century.[42] It was during this visit that the last recorded miracle took place at St Cuthbert's shrine, one of her gentlemen, Richard Poele, being cured of a rupture. The fascination of the shrine was dying away. Offerings, which had been great both in number and value, dwindled until by 1514 they had ceased altogether.

## 11
## 'THE OLD FLOURISHING TIME'

A vivid description of the life of the monastery in its last days was produced about 1593, possibly by George Bates, the last registrar of the house. Different versions of it were added to later. No doubt the author had written sources to which he could refer for the history, and perhaps for some of the descriptions, but it is, in the main, the product of an old man's memory lingering with pride and affection over every detail of the past, which was more real to him than the present. It is now known as *The Rites of Durham*.[43] Reading it, the great abbey lives again. A visitor entering at the North Door, must have been overwhelmed by a blaze of colour. Traces of painting, still on the walls, suggest that the interior of the church was decorated with bold designs in black and red. Every window was filled with brilliantly coloured glass, in which were depicted the histories of apostles and saints. Facing him, as he turned east, would be the

Jesus altar, which stood between the two furthest pillars of the nave. Behind it ran a wall, which went the whole breadth of the church. On it was carved the story of Christ

'very curiously and excellently finely gilt with branches and flowers, the more that a man did look on it the more was his affection to behold it—Upon the wall did stand the most goodly and famous rood that was in all the land—so what for the fairness of the wall, the stateliness of the pictures, and the livelihood of the painting, it was thought to be one of the goodliest monuments in that church'.[44]

Mass was said there on Fridays, and on principal days a triptych was opened, on which was painted and gilded the passion of Our Lord. Doors on either side, which were locked at night, led through to the crossing under the lantern. Three bells hung there; and four men, whose duty it was to ring the bells for the services, to keep the church clean, look after the vestments, and fill the holy water stoups every Sunday, lived in two chambers near by.

The choir, entered through a door in the carved stone screen, was dominated by the high altar, with Hatfield's chantry, another blaze of colour on the South Side. The altar was hung with red velvet 'wrought with great flowers in gold, and embroidered work' except on the feast of the Assumption, when it was 'all white damask, set with pearls and precious stones'. Over the centre of the altar a canopy for the Blessed Sacrament hung above the pyx, on which was a tall silver pelican piercing her breast to give blood to her young, as 'a symbol of Christ's blood which is given for the sins of the world'. A lectern, from which the Epistle and Gospel were sung, stood at the North End of the altar. It also was in the form of a pelican piercing her breast, but was made of brass, finely gilded. An eagle lectern stood further down the choir, from which the cantors sung the offices.

Doors on either side of the high altar led through to St Cuthbert's shrine, which was the heart of the whole church. It stood in the centre of a platform, which jutted out into the chapel of the Nine Altars. The coffin itself rested on a pedestal of green and gold marble, with four places in front of it, specially designed for the lame and the sick to rest in, while they prayed St Cuthbert to cure them. At the West End of the shrine, with its back to the Neville Screen, stood a little altar, on which Mass was said on St Cuthbert's day. The coffin itself had a wooden cover, gilded and painted, which was drawn up when the coffin was to be exposed, by a rope running through a pulley in the vault and having on it six silver bells, which, as they moved, called all who were in the church to come and make their prayers to God and St Cuthbert. To the north and south of the shrine were cupboards for all the mass of relics and special gifts which had accumulated there. When Richard de Segbrok, a careful man, was made shrine-keeper in 1383, he made a list of all the articles in his charge. It contains a bewildering assortment of hair, ashes, bones of saints, and fragments of their clothing, most of it displayed in reliquaries of crystal, ivory, or silver-gilt. There were a griffin's eggs and claws, pictures, precious stones, books of special value or having some particular connection, richly-made crucifixes, a rib and some of the milk of the Virgin Mary; a list which detailed the grotesque hoard of centuries including 'a pyx of black crystal, containing the sponge, and a piece of the sepulchre of the Lord, and of the stone upon which Jesus sat in the judgement seat of Herod. A piece of the tree, under which were the three angels with Abraham' is given, side by side, with 'a beryl, white and hollow, of wonderful structure'.[45]

In the past, a considerable part of the abbey's wealth, had come from offerings made by the stream of pilgrims. When any important person arrived who desired to see St Cuthbert's coffin, or a special gift was to be made, the monk in charge of the shrine had to get the permission of his superior, who came with the keys and watched while the cover was drawn up, replaced, and locked again. If Bates was the author of the *Rites* he was himself, as a young man in charge of the shrine.

At the other end of the abbey, in a room over the North Door, two men were always on duty, waiting to receive those who claimed sanctuary in the church. Anyone, no matter what his crime, if he knocked on the door with the great bronze knocker, which still fascinates visitors, would be let in at any hour of the day or night. As soon as he entered, he had to go to the Galilee and toll the bell, to let everyone know that there was a man who claimed sanctuary. The prior would then order the fugitive to keep within the church or the churchyard, and to wear a gown of black cloth, with a yellow cross of St Cuthbert on his left shoulder. The prior would then allow him to live at the expense of the monastery for thirty-seven days, until his case was decided. During the period 1464 to 1524, 247 persons claimed sanctuary.[46] They were of all classes, and accused of every kind of crime, with homicide predominating in that violent age.

The proceedings with a man called Colson from the village of Wolsingham, a few miles away, may be given as an example. He was a thief who had escaped from prison and claimed sanctuary. He stood before St Cuthbert's shrine, and asked for a coroner, who went to him and heard him confess his crime. The culprit then, by a solemn oath, renounced the kingdom. He stripped himself to his shirt and gave his clothes to the sacrist as a fee. The sacrist then gave them back to him, with a white wooden cross to hold in his hand. He was then put into the custody of the under-sheriff, who passed him from constable to constable, until he reached the coast, and was sent on board a ship, never to return.

Music had a great place in the daily worship. To provide for this there was a song-school at the South End of the Nine Altars, where a master taught six singing boys. It was his duty to play the organ at High Mass and at Vespers on the principal days; at the night offices one of the monks played. There were three of these organs. The best was over the door, in the choir-screen, and was only used on the principal feasts. Its pipes were of the finest wood, beautifully carved and gilded with a design of branches and flowers and the name of Jesus. There were only two others like it in England, one at York and the other in London, at St Paul's. Another organ called 'the cryers' stood on the North Side of the choir and was played only when lessons from St Augustine, St Gregory, St Ambrose, or St Jerome were read. There was a bell called 'the cryer', and possibly it took its name from that, because of its bell-like tone. The third organ was in daily use. Every Friday night, after Vespers were finished in the choir, the master and his pupils sang an anthem before the Jesus altar, for the benefit of those who were in the nave. When that was done, the boys sang an anthem by themselves, also before the Jesus altar, and one of the bells in the Galilee was rung at the same time. The master also played the organ, and the boys assisted by the deacons, sang the Mass at the altar of Our Lady in the Galilee every day. For a great part of the time, the church must have been filled with music and prayer. On festival days, there was the pomp of processions, with the display of all that was glorious among their treasures. Chief among these, was the great paschal, which was set up in the choir from Maundy Thursday until the Wednesday after Ascension Day. It was almost the breadth of the choir, and reached up to the vault. Decorated with crystals and dragons, and 'curious antic work, as beasts and men upon horseback, with bucklers, bows, and shafts, and knots with broad leaves spread upon the knots, very finely wrought, all being of most fine and curious candlestick metal',[47] with seven candles, the topmost being lit 'by a fine conveyance' through the roof of the church; it was thought to be 'one of the rarest monuments in all England'.

Apart from the daily offices, the working day began in the chapter house, where, after Prime in summer and Terce in winter, all the monks were gathered. Saints, martyrs, and local benefactors were commemorated, work was distributed to the monks, a chapter of the Rule was read and expounded, and faults confessed, before they all dispersed to their work in the cloisters. Since it was cold there in the winter time, a fire was kept in the Common House, just off the cloisters, so that the monks could drop in from time to time and warm themselves. On the West Side of the cloisters, the novices were taught, morning and afternoon; the master sat with his back to the cloister garth, and his pupils in front of him; the porter had strict orders to see that they were not disturbed. If they were well behaved, they were allowed to play bowls occasionally in the bowling alley, to the west of the main buildings, above the river bank.

At eleven o'clock a bell rang, and the monks went to wash before the midday meal. This was done in a round building at the South End of the cloister garth, with a dovecote above it and lit by seven windows. Inside was a marble basin with twenty-four brass taps. Each monk had a little cupboard, well ventilated, in which to keep his towel. By the sixteenth century the main body of the monks had left the refectory to the novices and their master; they now took their meals in the smaller room which had originally been meant for the old and ailing, no doubt because the food was better there. Each monk had his own mazer bowl, and there were also the great mazers 'edged about with silver and double gilt', including St Bede's bowl, which had a picture of the saint in the bottom, as he had been at his studies. When they had finished their meal, the monks went into the cemetery at the South End of the Nine Altars and stood for a while, bareheaded, in prayer and meditation among the tombs. Then the older men went to the North Side of the cloister, which was glazed in; there each had his cubicle; just big enough to hold a seat and a desk, where he could catch what sun there was, read, and no doubt doze a little, until Vespers at three o'clock.

Supper was at five o'clock, after which they went to the chapter house again to meet the prior. All doors were locked at six, and stayed so until seven the next morning. In the dormitory every monk had his own chamber with a little window, where there was room enough for a bed and a desk; the novices were more uncomfortable, for their quarters were at the South End of the dormitory, where windows were impossible. A marble pavement ran down the middle. A little before midnight, when mattins was due to be said, the sub-prior, who slept by the exit at the North End, made the rounds and called the name of each monk outside his door, to make sure that he was where he ought to be and that nothing untoward was going on. At night, the dormitory was filled with flickering light and shadow by twelve cressets at either end; each group flaming and smoking in a hollowed stone, which was kept filled with fat by the cook.

The guest hall, under the care of the hostillar, must have provided many contacts with the wider world. It offered

'entertainment to all states, both noble and gentle, and what degree so ever, that came thither as strangers, their entertainment not being inferior to any place in England, both for the goodness of their diet, the sweet and dainty furniture of their lodgings, and generally all things necessary for travellers, and withal this entertainment continuing, not willing, nor commanding, any man to depart upon his honest and good behaviour'.[48]

Durham maintained to the end the tradition of hospitality, which had largely died out in other places. Down by the great gate of the abbey, was a school for poor children, one or two of whom fetched food for them all from the novices' table. Four old women had a room each near by and were fed from the prior's table; they had a priest to say Mass for them every Friday and holy day. Scattered about the abbey premises were the offices of the men in charge of all the varied needs of the community, who consisted of the chamberlain, the bursar, the cellarer, the keeper of the garner, the other officials already mentioned, and many more besides. The life, ordered and gracious, an oasis of civilization in the rough existence of the time, went steadily on its routine; this was broken only by the ceremonies of festival days, with their little feasts, like that on *O Sapientia*, which came between Martinmas and Christmas; when the prior and his monks had a treat of 'figs and raisins, ale and cakes, and thereof no superfluity or excess, but a scholastical and moderate congratulation among themselves'.[49] It is no wonder that an old man who had been driven out of it looked back on it with pride and sadness, as 'the old flourishing time'.

But it was to come to an end. There was no longer much public sympathy for it. The feeling was growing that monasticism had had its day. People were demanding that religious persons should be fully committed to the life of ordinary men and women in the world. To the authorities monasteries were obnoxious, as bastions against change. Men with power, from the King downward, looked enviously at their wealth. A visitation of the monasteries was followed in 1536 by the suppression of religious houses with an income of less than £200 a year. Under it Durham lost its outlying cells, and their monks were withdrawn to the parent house, swelling the numbers there to about seventy. Wolsey had taken the bishoprick in 1522; but though he interfered in the secular concerns of the diocese, he never visited it, and moved to Winchester in 1529. An attack on the larger monasteries quickly followed the destruction of the smaller ones.

We do not know the exact date when the King's commissioners, Dr Leigh, Dr Henley, and Dr Blitheman visited Durham, but we have a vivid account of their actions at the shrine.[50] They brought jewellers with them, who went through the vast accumulation of treasure, which had built up through the years. Everything of any value was taken, including one stone, an emerald, said to be worth a king's ransom. It had been valued in 1401, with five rings and silver chains, at £3336 13s 4d.[51] Because it is never mentioned by the commissioners afterwards, it has been suggested that it was spurious, but if that had been so, it would have been widely proclaimed as another instance of monkish fraud. It is more likely that it never reached the King, but was quietly disposed of. The commissioners proceeded to open the various coffins which held the body of St Cuthbert. One of them was so strongly bound with iron that the goldsmith, who was doing the work, had to break it open with a sledge-hammer. He found the body lying 'whole, uncorrupt, with his face bare, and his beard as it had been a fortnight's growth and all his vestments upon him, as he was accustomed to say Mass withal, and his metwand[52] of gold lying beside him'. The goldsmith was dismayed to find that he had broken one of the saint's legs, and called out to the commissioners below to that effect. He was, no doubt, on the top of the pedestal, and the commissioners standing on the floor of the shrine. Dr Henley ordered him to throw down the bones, and the man said that he could not, for they were all held together by the sinews and the skin. Dr Leigh then went up to look, and called down to Dr Henley in Latin that the body was lying whole. Henley did not believe it, and still said, 'cast down the bones'. Leigh answered, 'If you will not believe me, come up yourself and see him'. So he went up, and handled the body, and found that not only it, but the vestments, were 'fresh, safe, and not consumed'.

Nothing emphasizes more the change which had taken place, than the attitude of the commissioners to a relic which had for so long been reckoned almost too sacred to look at, let alone touch. They ordered the coffin to be taken into an inner vestry, and kept safe until the King's pleasure should be known. It lay there for a while, until permission was given for it to be buried, which the monks did, making the grave on the very spot where the shrine had stood.[53] The various remains of other saints must have been preserved also, for they were found in 1827 in the same grave with St Cuthbert. Bede's shrine was destroyed as well, and his bones like those of St Cuthbert, buried beneath the place where it had been.

The last prior was Hugh Whitehead, who succeeded Prior Castell after a five-year vacancy. He was a learned man who had been head of Durham College, Oxford, and was venerated for his deeply religious character. There was no scandal reported among the Durham monks, and it is unlikely that it would have gone without mention if there had been any. On 31 December 1539, Whitehead and his brethren surrendered the abbey into the King's hands. Its revenues at that time were estimated by Dugdale at £1366 10s 5d, and by Speed at £1615 14s 10d.[54] Until a fresh arrangement could be made, Whitehead was to be in charge. All debts were to be paid, and all unnecessary servants discharged, with six months' wages. Mattins was to be said at six o'clock in the morning, and the customary Mass of Our Lady continued according to the Use of Sarum which, although we cannot be sure, had probably been the practice at Durham.

# 2

# *The Reformation*

## 1

## THE NEW AGE BEGINS

On 12 May 1541 King Henry VIII, intending, as he said, that the
sacred oracles and sacraments should be purely administered, honest
morals established, youth trained in letters, and provision made for
the old age of those who had served him well, refounded Durham
as the Cathedral Church of Christ and the Blessed Virgin Mary,
with a dean and twelve prebendaries. They were to see that the poor
were cared for, and roads and bridges repaired 'to the glory of God
and the happiness of our subjects'.[1] The abbey and its estates were
given back to them, with a yearly charge on them of £218 to the
king, and a long list of financial obligations belonging to the former
monastery, which were still to be observed. The set of model statutes,
which were sent to most of the other cathedrals of the new foundation, either never reached Durham or have disappeared, for there is
no trace of them now. The former prior, Hugh Whitehead, was made
dean, and the twelve prebendaries had all been members of the old
establishment. The rest were given places in various churches about
the bishoprick.

The break came when both the Prior and the Bishop, who was not
directly involved in the surrender of the monastery, were as
distinguished as any in the history of Durham. Cuthbert Tunstall
had been translated there from London in 1530 by a papal bull, the
last to be issued in England for such a purpose. He had studied at
both Oxford and Cambridge, as well as at universities on the
continent, and represented the best of both the new and the old
learning. Erasmus was his friend, and like Erasmus, he did not find
it easy to take sides, which was a handicap for both of them in days
when a man was suspect unless he was a violent partisan. He kept
the see through all the changes from Henry VIII to Elizabeth and
might have been a moderating influence, if anybody had been in-

clined to be moderate. Within the cathedral there was no destruction and probably not much change, so long as Whitehead was in charge. But to the hot reformers of Edward VI's reign, he was bound to seem at best lukewarm, and possibly compromised in one way or another. Together with Bishop Tunstall and the subdean, Dr Hyndman, Whitehead was summoned before the King's Council in 1548. Worried at what might happen, and worn out with travelling, he died soon after he arrived in London, and was buried in Holy Trinity church in the Minories. It is possible that he might have had a hand in an attempt at Durham to preserve some of the monks' possessions from the general wreck, for on 11 August 1550 Sir R. Bowes and Sir J. Hilton informed the Privy Council that a great quantity of treasure had been conveyed into the dean of Durham's chamber, though there is no indication of what happened as a result.[2]

Three years later Whitehead was succeeded by Robert Horne, a good scholar and a radical reformer, who was bitterly opposed to the old regime. He began the work of destruction by smashing up a good deal of the stained glass and by removing the effigy of St Cuthbert, which had lain in an elaborate shrine in the cloisters, on the spot where the body itself had been kept, until its removal to a place behind the high altar. Visitors to the cathedral would see changes. English, of course, took the place of Latin in the services, but to the great number of Durham people who used a broad Northumbrian dialect, Cranmer's literary English must have been hardly more understandable, and much less familiar in sound, than the old language. Horne and Tunstall would not be likely to get on together, and with the change of direction when Mary came to the throne, it was not surprising that the Bishop made an effort to get rid of him. He was summoned before the Privy Council and accused of a medley of faults, including interfering with the work of the Bishop, preaching heresy, being a Scot, and 'being dean of Durham brought a wife into the church, where never woman came before'.[3] He was ejected and joined the Protestant exiles in Frankfurt, where, none the less, he took a leading part among those who supported episcopacy.

For the next four years Thomas Watson, the Master of St John's College, Cambridge, a 'warm Roman Catholic and a great favourite of Cardinal Pole' was dean, and something like the old fashion of things came back to the cathedral. The monastery was not refounded, but on 20 March 1554/5 Philip and Mary issued statutes for Durham Cathedral under the Great Seal, which were based on those which had been drawn up for the new cathedrals in Henry VIII's time. They remained in force until recently, and form the basis of those which still operate. The bishop was to take precedence of the dean and chapter, and was to be received with all proper ceremony when he came to the cathedral. He had, however, no place on the capitular body, and could exercise authority only when he appeared as the statutory visitor. The statutes were designed

> 'not to subject the cathedral body to the authority of the bishop, but to provide the see, liable in the natural course of things to recurring vacancies and other casualties, with a permanent body of trustees, to whom its temporary occupant was responsible'.[4]

The dean was to be appointed by the Crown, and not elected by the chapter, as in the monastic days, and was to be the undisputed head; but in all business affecting the common good, he was to be subject to the agreement of the chapter, in which the prebendaries exercised their corporate rights, though they had none as individuals. Respect for the new body was to be insured by the insistence that the prebendaries were to be priests of good life, without heresy, and at least bachelors of laws of one of the universities. The dean was not to live 'sordidly', but keep a regular family, and live according to his dignity. If he failed in this, he was to be reproved by the bishop.

Music was provided for by an establishment of sixteen singing men and ten choristers with their master. There was to be a grammar school, with two masters and eighteen scholars, a divinity reader, twelve minor canons, a deacon and subdeacon, eight almsmen, with two vergers, two sextons, two porters, two cooks, and two barbers. The need for the cooks is explained by the regulation that the unmarried minor canons, deacons, and clerks should mess together in the common hall, sitting, without distinction of place, under the presidency of the precentor or the senior minor canon, an arrangement which lasted well into the seventeenth century. The singing men and the master of the choristers, with his boys, were to assist every day at divine service, except for Evensong, and every one of them was to be in a surplice or his proper vestment. The grammar scholars were to be in church on all festival days, wearing surplices and under the direction of the precentor. It was a pattern of life which was to persist in all its main features through more than three centuries. All these were found accommodation in the old monastic buildings.

The accession of Elizabeth brought Robert Horne back to the

deanery, to do a little more destruction before he was made bishop of Winchester in 1560. He was a stout reformer, but loyal to the Church of England, and, in Fuller's opinion, was 'constantly ground between two opposite parties, Papists and Sectaries ... both twitted his person as dwarfish and deformed, to which I say nothing, save that such taunts carp at the case, when they cannot find fault with the jewel'.[5] For the next three years Ralph Skinner, the master of Sherburn Hospital, was dean. Under Chapter 18 of the Statutes estates were assigned to the dean and each of the prebendaries, and other sums were added to these later on. The proceeds of the woods, mines, and quarries were to provide for the general purposes of the cathedral, and to this the dean was to contribute £10 4s a year, and the prebendaries in proportion to their income. Any surplus in the general fund was to be divided among them at regular audits. No doubt the division was fair enough at first, though there must always have been differences due to the different quality of land involved. Later on, however, there were great inequalities, as mining developments on some estates made their owners immensely wealthy. At the start the dean's estate brought in £284 4s 8d a year, the average for the prebendaries was £32 5s 10d. The divinity reader had £20 a year, the schoolmaster £11, the minor canons £10 each, and the master of the choristers £9 10s.[6] Obviously the deanery was worth having and, as it was without cure of souls, when Skinner died in 1563, Queen Elizabeth proposed to give it to Thomas Wilson, a layman, one of her secretaries. She was, on this occasion, however, persuaded to change her mind, and on account of his great merits to give it to William Whittingham.

Whittingham was a dramatic figure, even in the colourful history of Durham; he was that combination of soldier and man of God which was so dear to the puritan heart.[7] Like so many of his predecessors he was a learned man, having been a Fellow of All Souls College, Oxford, and one of the first seniors created in Henry VIII's new college of Christ Church. He had studied in the university of Orleans and married there a sister, (it is said) of John Calvin. A brief visit to England was brought to an end by the accession of Queen Mary; he then went to Frankfurt, and thence to Geneva, where Calvin persuaded him to give up the idea of a secular career and become a minister. He had a share in the translation of the Breeches Bible (so-called because it said that Adam made himself 'breeches' of fig leaves), and contributed seven psalms to the rough but vigorous translation put out by Sternhold and Hopkins, which

44

became the song book of the Reformation, voicing, as it did, the hopes and fears of puritan England. On his return home he went as chaplain to the Earl of Warwick, commander of the English forces in the defence of Le Havre, or Neuhaven, against the French. He not only ministered to the spiritual needs of the garrison, but took his part in the fighting, 'preaching in his armour continually'. When an alarm came in sermon time 'he would be on the town walls as soon as any man'. He was the means of discovering a stratagem of the French to take the town, and was conspicuous not only for his valour but also for his devotion in ministering to 'so many soldiers dying and dead of the plague, in one great room'.[8] It was for these services that the Queen gave him the deanery.

In Durham a good many people liked him, for he was a hospitable man and one who did his duty faithfully, as he saw it. Writing to Sir William Cecil, the Queen's secretary, he says that because the grammar school was without an able master, he taught the boys himself for three or four hours every day. There was half-an-hour's worship in the cathedral every morning at six o'clock, for the servants, the school boys, and the song school. Mattins was said at nine o'clock, and Evensong at three in the afternoon. On Wednesdays and Fridays, there was a general fast with prayer and preaching; and on Sundays and holy days, there was a sermon in the morning and catechizing in the afternoon.[9] Religion was certainly not being neglected in Durham, though it was being expressed in new ways.

2

## THE RISING IN THE NORTH

To the author of the *Rites*, Whittingham was the arch-enemy, the great destroyer, and it was almost inevitable that it should be so. 'He could not abide anything that pertained to the monastical life'.[10] He had all the carvings defaced, and got rid of all the brasses, especially those with any imagery on them. The holy water stoups and memorial stones, were put to use in his kitchen and stables. To him they were monuments of idolatry, which had not only to be removed but also degraded, lest any superstitious reverence should still cling to them. His wife burned the famous Banner of St Cuthbert on 'her fire, in notable contempt and disgrace of all ancient and goodly reliques'.[11] Priceless works of art were destroyed at the Whittinghams' hands. We may regret the vandalism, but all revolu-

45

tionaries have the urge to eliminate the symbols of the past from which they seek to break away. In a religious, as in a political, revolution, irreparable damage to things of value in themselves is the price paid for escape from the system which produced them. Whittingham was accused of making a profit of £20 for himself by taking down the high leaden roof of the refectory and replacing it with a flat one. It was also said that he intended to sell the peal of four bells which hung in the steeple of the Galilee, and was only prevented from doing so by Thomas Spark, the suffragan bishop, who caused three of them to be moved into the central tower at his own expense. But as these charges are made by the author of the *Rites*, they should perhaps be received with some hesitation. After her husband's death, Mrs Whittingham built a house in the Bailey, using stones from the old cemetery garth, two of the best being laid down as thresholds. When the house had passed into other hands, an old man 'with comely grey hairs' came begging, and seeing the stones, said that the house would never prosper while they were there; he went away without accepting anything and soon afterwards seven children of the household died. The stones were therefore put back in the churchyard.[12] Things which had been sacred only a few years before were now being used everywhere for common purposes.

The first result of the Reformation was to produce chaos in the economic, as well as the ecclesiastical and spiritual, life of England. Popular preachers, like Bishop Latimer and Bernard Gilpin, the Apostle of the North, inveighed against both social and spiritual evils; the two seemed to them inseparable. The barriers were down; everybody was grabbing what he could, while the poor and those without powerful friends were being crushed in the struggle. The Church had been kind to them but the Church was now suffering as much as they were. If poverty is a virtue in the clergy, every layman who had the chance was doing his best to promote it. The bishop, James Pilkington, was a strong Protestant, one of the exiles who had come back, to receive high office under Elizabeth. Bishop Tunstall, who had survived all the changes from Henry VIII until the death of Mary, had found himself unable to take the oath which declared Elizabeth the supreme governor of the Church of England, and had been deprived of his see in July 1559; he lived for the four months which were all that he had left in this world more as the guest than as the prisoner of Archbishop Parker. Everything seemed to increase the nostalgia for the old days and the religion which went with it. The greed of patrons, who either farmed their livings, or

46

kept them in their own hands, giving 'some three-halfpenny priest a curate's wages, nine or ten pounds a year', to do the duty, left the people without anyone to instruct them in the new approach to religion.

> They come to church to feast their eyes, and not their souls; they are not taught that no visible thing is to be worshipped. And so, because they see not in the church the shining pomp and pleasant variety (as they thought it) of painted clothes, candlesticks, images, altars, lamps, tapers, they say 'as good go into a barn'.[13]

As the result of a mass of confused loyalties and discontents, the Rising in the North broke out in 1569, headed by the Earls of Westmorland, and Northumberland. Whittingham had word of what was brewing and warned the Bishop, but Pilkington refused to do anything, on the rather curious ground that he had a great deal of the Queen's money in his care. But if the Bishop would not move, the Dean would. A soldier once more, he went to Newcastle and exhorted the Mayor and Aldermen to prepare the town for a siege, and when they accepted his advice, he showed them how to do it, out of his experience at Neuhaven. As a result, Newcastle was never taken, but the rebels occupied Durham without opposition. They tore and defaced the English-language Bibles and service books in the cathedral and if that was necessary forced some of its clergy to celebrate Mass according to the old order. Mr John Brimley, whose tomb can still be seen in the Galilee, and who was then the master of the choristers, played the organ for the Mass, explaining later on that he only did so under compulsion; though not much of that can have been needed, for he went in procession, knelt to be reconciled, and 'bade others do so'.[14] His attitude was probably much the same as that of the others. The rising, the last in England of the old feudal type of rebellion, never stood a chance of success, and was put down with great savagery. It had added one more element of danger, to the beleaguered Mary Queen of Scots, who, as a Roman Catholic and heir presumptive to the English throne, was suspected of having a hand in it, though she probably had none.

During the rebellion Whittingham was with his old commander, the Earl of Warwick who, with the Earl of Lincoln, was in charge of the Queen's forces. Pilkington was forced to keep out of the way. He had got together a great fortune, and later on, gave his two daughters £4000 each as marriage portions; a proceeding which so enraged Queen Elizabeth that she took £1000 a year away from the bishoprick, and used it for the support of the garrison at Berwick. This was not an unreasonable proceeding, when it is remembered that it had been a part of the bishop's duty to guard the border. Pilkington's death in 1576 brought the old dispute about the power of the archbishop of York to the fore again. Barnes, the new bishop, proposed to visit the cathedral as the archbishop's deputy, but Whittingham told him that he wronged both himself and the bishoprick by doing so, and when he arrived at the chapter house door, he had it locked in his face. Barnes tried to force his way in, but the Dean 'did interrupt him a little, taking hold of his gown'.[15] This brought a whole storm of complaints down on Whittingham's head. The Bishop obtained a commission from the Privy Council, which visited Durham, and examined into fifty articles against the Dean, among them that he was not properly ordained, and that he was ineligible for his office, as he was only a master of arts, while the statutes demanded that he should be a bachelor of divinity, at least. The commission allowed this charge, but brushed aside the others. Whittingham produced a certificate to the effect that, while he was in Geneva, 'it pleased God by lot, and election of the whole English congregation, to choose him to the office of preaching';[16] and claimed that Geneva orders had been accepted in England until the eighth year of Queen Elizabeth's reign, four years after his appointment. Whittingham was harassed a good deal, but kept his place. Sandys, the archbishop of York, complained that, 'The dean hath gotten more friends than the matter deserveth'.[17] Whittingham's popularity in Durham was increased rather than injured by the attack. Frustrated, Bishop Barnes could only grumble that the church at Durham was an Augean stable, 'whose stink is grievous in the nose of God and man', and which it was beyond his power to cleanse. Most people said that the real cause of offence at Durham was Barnes' brother, the chancellor of the diocese, who had made his consistory court (which sat in the Galilee) a by-word for oppression and injustice. In 1577 the disputes between the chapter and their tenants over leases grew so bitter that the Queen was forced to intervene, and settle the rights of both parties.

After Whittingham's death in 1579, the layman, Thomas Wilson, at last got the deanery. He had written learnedly on logic and rhetoric and was said to have suffered in the Inquisition when in Rome, for heresy which he had somehow managed to insinuate in those subjects. He was afterwards Secretary of State and a Privy Councillor, but he never visited Durham, and his duties were carried out by the Subdean. Durham settled down under the deans who succeeded Wilson. They managed to get on with the successive bishops, and avoided too much scandal. They were learned men who were serviceable to the Crown; two of them, Tobias Matthew and William James, each went on the bishoprick. In 1606 James I appointed another layman, Adam Newton, who had been tutor to Prince Henry. He also never came near Durham and had his duties performed by a rather reluctant subdean, until he was bought out in 1620.

## 3
## THE LAUDIAN REACTION

Changes were taking place in the theological thinking of the time. The action and reaction which persists through all ecclesiastical history, was having its effects. Men who wished to combine the best in the old and the new systems were beginning to make themselves heard. With the arrival in 1617 of the much translated Richard Neil in the bishoprick (he had already passed through three dioceses, and was to go on to two more including the archbishoprick of York) the new outlook reached Durham. The old wooden Lord's Table, which had done duty since the Reformation, was removed from the centre of the choir, where the people had gathered round it, to the East End and placed altar-wise. The new dean, Richard Hunt, who succeeded Newton, was from Trinity College, Cambridge, and was followed by a considerable importation of Cambridge men, all of whom were more or less in touch with Laud. The most distinguished of the group, John Cosin, was to have a long and famous connection with the cathedral and the see. The alarm with which the protestant stalwarts at Durham saw this invasion can hardly have been allayed when, in 1627, three years after his arrival, Cosin published his *Private Devotions*, a book of which the catholic temper brought the puritan pamphleteers down upon him with a howl of fury. The pent-up anger at Durham burst out on Sunday 27 July 1628, when Peter Smart, the prebendary preaching that day, made his sermon a vitriolic attack on the new High Church ways, with Cosin and Hunt particularly in mind. Smart had come to Durham in 1598 as master of the grammar school. Bishop James had favoured him a good deal and had given him a stall in the cathedral, with much other valuable preferment. The natural suspicion between the old country schoolmaster and 'the young Apollo', 'the curled Adonis from Cambridge', could only be heightened when one was grimly puritan, and the other determined to set a new High Church stamp on everything. Trouble was bound to come.

Smart began well enough, taking for his text, 'I hate them that hold of superstitious vanities, but thy law do I love,'[18] explaining that it was not the man, but the sin that they hated; but he warmed up as he went along, and began to refer to a young man, who was introducing all sorts of wicked practices.

> 'Before we had ministers, as the Scripture calls them, we had Communion Tables, we had sacraments, but now we have priests and sacrifices and altars, with much altar furniture, and many massing implements. Nay, what want we? Have we not all religion again? For if religion consists in altar-ducking, cope-wearing, organ-playing, piping and singing, crossing of cushions, and kissing of clouts, oft starting up and squatting down, nodding of heads, and whirling about, till their noses stand Eastward, setting basons on the altar, candlesticks and crucifixes, burning wax candles in excessive number when and where there is no use of lights, and that which is worst of all, gilding of angels and garnishing of images, and setting them aloft—if, I say religion consist in these and such like superstitious vanities, ceremonial fooleries, apish toys, and popish trinkets, we never had more religion than now.'[19]

His advice to the congregation was, 'Stay at home in the name of God till things be amended'.

Stung by the attack, the Dean called a meeting for two o'clock on the same Sunday afternoon. They met in 'the great chamber' of the deanery, probably either the present dining room or drawing room, and called upon Smart to repent for his 'seditious' sermon. They were not meeting as a chapter, but as the Durham section of the Court of High Commission. In the previous March that very court had already complained of Cosin for the candles, (there were said to be 340 of them) and for the painting and gilding that he had carried out in the choir, glancing at the Bishop of Durham 'whom Cosin wholely ruleth', for being behind it all.

The struggle begun that Sunday afternoon dragged on for years. It was just one conspicuous part of the dispute which was going on all over England. Smart was suspended from his prebend, and the income sequestrated; but he stubbornly sat on in chapter, as a protest against robbing him of his rights. He immediately published

2 Boss in the vaulting of the choir. Abraham's bosom

3 Head of a prior, possibly Thomas Melsonby, in the chapel of the Nine Altars

1 Choir in the mid-eighteenth century

5 Tomb of St Cuthbert

4 Tomb of the Venerable Bede

the offending sermon, with an appendix in which he named Cosin and detailed the charges against him, adding that Cosin had said that, 'The king is no more head of the Church of England than the man that rubs my horse's heels'. The old charge about the candles was elaborated into running up and down ladders all Candlemas Day and lighting 220 of them, sixty near the altar, with sixteen torches. Cosin, he claimed, had made everybody turn East at the Creed, and re-introduced the medieval copes, which had previously only been used in 'May Day games'. He had also brought in tunes from the Mass Book, with organs, sackbuts, and cornets. Smart's obsessive dislike of music and singing can only have been increased by the fact that three months before his famous sermon, the dean and chapter had been forced to reprimand their organist, an outstanding musician called Richard Hutchinson, for 'frequent haunting of alehouses, and other evil demeanours',[20] and particularly for breaking the head of Toby Broking, one of the singing men of the church, with a candlestick in an alehouse, and wounding him very dangerously. They threatened to expel Hutchinson if he did not amend.

Smart was letting his wrath get the better of him, for he claimed that the new marble altar, recently set up in the East End, had cost £3000, a wild exaggeration, for the price was nearer £200. He also made a vicious attack on Bishop Neil, which he published in A Short Treatise of Altars,[21] claiming that Neil had been a school-fellow of his and a notorious ignoramus, who had cringed his way from bishopric to bishopric. Cosin defended himself strongly, especially against the charge that he had spoken disrespectfully of the King, producing affidavits from friends, who had been present at the dinner when the words complained of had been allegedly spoken. The whole dispute is mainly of interest now for the light it throws on the changes which were taking place at Durham. The case was transferred to London, and London looked at it, and sent it back to York, where Smart was fined £500. When he failed to pay, he was committed to prison. His friends and even his wife thought that he had been too violent and obstinate, but he sat it out in prison from the end of 1629 until 1640, when a puritan parliament took his part. Meanwhile sympathizers saw that he did not want. Nobody minced their words in the quarrel. The High Churchmen called Smart, and his friends, 'Blasphemers of God and the king, Cains, chams,[22] Judases, seditious, and disobedient, persons'. The Puritans retorted, a little more succinctly, that 'The Durham chapter was a mangy pack of Arminian hellhounds'.

The new order of things, which so offended Smart, none the less appeared very attractive to some others. Three soldiers, a captain, a lieutenant, and an ancient (ensign), who passed through Durham in the autumn of 1634, were lyrical in their praise. Going to prayers in the cathedral, they 'were rapt with the sweet sound, and richness of a fair organ, and the devout and melodious singing of the choristers'. After the service, the Dean invited them to dinner, and finding that they came from Norfolk, his home county, gave them special attention, walking with them in the garden until the meal was ready. Before it was begun, a young scholar read a chapter, while all listened in silence, and then wine was served, to go with the 'fat venison, sweet salmon, and other great cheer'. When it was over, they parted from 'as good as free, and as generous a gentleman as England affords' with great regret.[23]

## 4
## ROYAL VISITS

Kings, too, found entertainment and little of which to complain in Durham. James I stayed a night there on his way south to receive the crown of England, and was feasted in the castle, attended by a hundred gentlemen, at the Bishop's expense. On his way north again in April 1617, he was once more entertained by the Bishop, this time at Auckland Castle, and from there signified his intention of entering Durham in state on Easter Eve. He was met on Elvet Bridge by the mayor, who presented him with a silver-gilt bowl; and after listening to an apprentice, who recited verses in his honour, was led by the Mayor, preceded by the city sword and mace, into the cathedral, to be received by the subdean and the prebendaries.[24]

In May 1633 Charles I, on his way to Scotland to be crowned, stayed a night with the Bishop at Auckland Castle. The next day, 1 June, he made a ceremonial entry into Durham, where he was met by the High-Sheriff, and the gentlemen of the county. As soon as he had alighted, he went straight to the cathedral. Considerable preparations had been made for him. A folio Prayer Book had been specially bound, in elaborate embroidery for his use and new copes made, one of which the cathedral still possesses. They were probably the work of local recusants, for one of the charges against Cosin was that he used them to supply vestments and altar breads. After saying the Lord's Prayer at the North Door, the King proceeded, under a canopy of state, carried by eight prebendaries in surplices, to a chair near the font in the second bay from the choir, on the South Side. There he listened to an address of welcome from Dean Hunt and joined in prayer for the success of his journey. After the singing of the Te Deum, he visited the tombs of St Cuthbert and the Venerable Bede and was presented with a rich cope, which he handed to Laud for use in the Royal Chapel, and received a petition for confirmation of the ancient rights of the cathedral. He spent the night at the castle. The next day he went to Mattins in the cathedral 'where none were admitted save his nobles, the clergy and the choir',[25] and heard a sermon by the Bishop. Afterwards, he dined at the deanery, though at the Bishop's expense, attended Evensong, and went back to the castle, where he touched several persons for the king's evil. Entertaining the royal party during their visit cost the bishop £1500 a day.

The next morning the chapter received a royal letter, drawing their attention to certain abuses which the King wished to have removed. Some 'mean tenements' in the churchyard were to be pulled down as soon as their leases had run out; and the chapter were to find seats for the mayor and corporation, the wives of the chapter, and 'other women of quality' somewhere else than in the choir. It is quite possible that a hint from Cosin was behind all this. The tenements were probably houses occupied by the singing men and the ancient sexton's office, built against the North Choir Aisle and then used as a song-school, may have been included, for it was pulled down in about 1633. Cosin was high in favour, for he was given the mastership of Peterhouse, Cambridge, and later the vice-chancellorship of that university; though at the King's wish he was still to receive his revenues from Durham, in spite of being unable to keep residence.

## 5
## TROUBLED TIMES

But circumstances were soon to change. There must have been a good deal of misery in Durham, even when national affairs were apparently normal. 'Pestilence' raged in the city from 1589, until 1604, and was endemic in the countryside for long after; whole populations left their towns, and villages, and camped on the moors to avoid its ravages.[26] The continual raiding, backwards and forwards across the Border, meant ruin for many. In the second Bishops' War of 1640, the ill-trained and semi-mutinous English army, which was to have imposed the King's will on Scotland, ran away after the defeat of their vanguard at Newburn-on-Tyne, and panic swept the neighbourhood. For four days after the battle, the shops in Durham were closed, and 'not one house in ten had man, woman, or child in it'. Hunger, if not famine, filled the city. The country people dared not come to market, and the English soldiers stole all the provisions, so that 'not one bit of bread could be got for money'.

In September 1640, the Scots occupied Durham and stayed until 1642. The dean, Walter Balcanquall, though himself a Scot, was obnoxious to his countrymen, and got out of the way. He had succeeded Hunt only the year before. The revenues of the cathedral were impounded to pay the cost of maintaining the invading army, whose reforming zeal overflowed into the church itself. They smashed the font, and began to wreck the organs; and when the dean's steward asked their general to interfere, he could do nothing but advise him to take the pipes out, which he did that night. The organ cases survived for a time.[27]

Peter Smart's dispute with the chapter, and Cosin particularly, had dragged on, and by this time practically everybody in England, who had any great authority, had come into it at some point or other. On 3 November 1640 the Long Parliament met for the first time, and on 10 November, Smart petitioned them for redress of his grievances. He was released from prison, and in the next year restored to his prebend. He went back to Durham, and spent the last years of his life wrangling about his debts, until he died at the age of 82 in 1652.

In 1646, the bishoprick of Durham was abolished, and its lands put up for sale. The bishop, Thomas Morton, after seeing his diocese devastated by the war, and being himself accused of high-treason, was on his way to London when he was overtaken by Sir Christopher Yelverton, who asked him who he was.

'I am that old man, the bishop of Durham, notwithstanding all your votes,' Morton replied. Asked where he was going, he said, 'To London, to live a little while, and then to die.'

Yelverton took him to his house, where he stayed for the next thirteen years, as tutor in the family, until his death when he was 95.[28] With the abolition of the bishoprick, the chapter was in difficulty too, and they were ordered to send their books to London for examination. They answered with a list of excuses, partly claiming that the books had been sent to Hull for safety, when the Scots were in Durham, and that they had then somehow got lost, and partly blaming their chapter clerk, but whatever the reason parliament never got the books.

In 1649 the dean and chapter of Durham were suppressed, and a good part of their lands sold by the state. Their tenants, who, in spite of disputes from time to time, were satisfied with their landlords, found themselves in trouble. Those who had no particular leases, but held their property because they, and their ancestors, had been on the abbey rent roll time out of mind, were faced with heavily increased charges or dispossessed.[29] Members of the cathedral establishment scattered to find bread and safety where they could. It was now Cosin's turn to suffer adversity. Harassed by parliament for his old dispute with Smart and his High-Church practices generally, he was deprived of all his preferment in the Church and at Cambridge, and withdrew to Paris in 1643. There, at the order of Charles I, he became chaplain to the Protestant members of Queen Henrietta-Maria's household, and did good work in ministering to exiles, and maintaining the position of the Church of England against Roman controversialists. The most romantic career was that of the archdeacon of Northumberland, Isaac Basire.[30] Of French extraction, he had been given considerable preferment in the Durham diocese, which was taken from him at the outbreak of the Civil War. Leaving his wife and children to do the best they could, he found refuge, first with the King at Oxford, and then overseas. For a while he travelled in Italy with a number of pupils and then, when they left him, went further afield. He was a good linguist and had the gift of making friends wherever he went. Travelling through the Morea and into Syria and Palestine, he went on to Aleppo and Constantinople, surviving among the Turks by his medical knowledge, which he had picked up when he was at Padua. When he could, he would write back home to his wife and send her a little money, if he had any; somehow, that indomitable woman managed to survive and keep her family. Basire himself made a point of studying, on the spot the different forms of faith among the ancient christian Churches, and explaining to them the true position of the Church of England. In 1654 he was invited to become the professor of divinity in the new university of Alba Julia on the borders of Hungary, which four years later was overrun by the Turks.

In June 1650 Oliver Cromwell passed through Durham on the way to his campaign in Scotland. On 3 September, he fought and won the battle of Dunbar, taking 3500 prisoners. These he sent back to Newcastle, charging Sir Arthur Hazelrigg, the governor there, to treat them with all humanity. Just how they were treated Sir Arthur describes in a letter to the Council of State on 31 October. When the prisoners reached Morpeth, they were turned loose in a large walled garden, filled with cabbages, which the starving men devoured, roots and all. They claimed that they had been without food for eight days, probably meaning that nothing had been issued to them and that they had lived as best they could. It is no wonder that many of them died on the road from Morpeth to Newcastle, where they were housed for the night in St Nicholas' church. The next morning, when they were sent on to Durham, 140 of them were too ill to march, and others died on the way there. In Durham they were herded into the cathedral; but the count as they went in, showed that there was now no more than 3000. Allowing for some who might have managed to slip away, the death roll on that disastrous march must have been very great. Sir Arthur Hazelrigg in his report claimed that the prisoners had received medical attention and all the help that they needed, but other accounts do not justify the claim. They were allowed no fuel, and the Durham autumn can be cold; the vast unheated cathedral became a death camp. They smashed up all the woodwork, including the remains of the organs, to feed their fires, the marks of which can still be seen. The only wooden thing which they left was the case of Prior Castell's great clock, some people suggest because it had on it a carving of the Scottish thistle, but a more probable reason might be that, cut off as they were, it might be some comfort to them to know the phases of the moon and the time of day. They took their revenge on the Nevilles for all that famous family had done against Scotland, by breaking up the alabaster tombs of Sir Ralph and Sir John. They were in charge of a man called Brewen, who was 'of bad character and a cruel fellow to the poor prisoners'. 'The ninth part' of the great paschal candlestick, which had been the glory of the church in the Middle Ages, had been 'thrown into an obscure place' at the Dissolution, and had been brought out again in the Laudian revival, for use as a lectern in the chancel, was finally stolen by Brewen. In spite of their hardships, enough of the prisoners survived to be sent south, and sold for slaves in New England, where they were not too badly treated; some of them founded families, which became important in the business community of Boston.[31]

# 6
## CROMWELL'S COLLEGE

Meanwhile the prebendaries' houses were deserted and falling into ruin. The lead had been taken from the former guest hall, and the building unroofed. All but one of the minor canons' houses had been destroyed. It seemed a pity that so great a property should go to waste. Accordingly, the Durham Grand Jury, on 7 May 1650, petitioned parliament that the houses of the dean and chapter should be used for a college for the benefit of the northern parts, which were so far from a university, and that their lands which were near the city, should be put to pious purposes. Parliament set up a committee to look into the matter. Cromwell had been approached and wrote to the Speaker, urging that a scheme for 'a college or school for all sciences and literature' should be drawn up, on the ground that it 'would much conduce to the promoting of learning and piety, in the poor, rude, and ignorant parts; there being also many concurring advantages to this place, as pleasantness and aptness of situation, healthful air, and plenty of provisions'. Encouraged by the interest aroused, the Durham Grand Jury wrote again, pointing out that the government owed the county £25,633 13s 10d of the money which they had been forced to find for the maintenance of the Scots army when it was among them, and asking that a competent revenue should be granted to the college on that account.

This also was referred to the committee, who reported that the dean and chapter property was suitable for a college. It took a little time to bring about, but in 1656 the Privy Council issued an order for founding the college in the cathedral precincts and endowing it with church lands, and on 15 May 1657, letters patent were issued for the purpose. The establishment was to consist of a provost, two senior fellows or preachers, twelve other fellows, of whom four were to be professors, four tutors, and four schoolmasters. There were to be twenty-four scholars, twelve exhibitioners, and eighteen pupils in the free school, attached to the college. The people who were to hold these offices were all named, and were men of ability. They were to be endowed with whatever property of the former dean and chapter remained unsold, as well as the cathedral building and the houses belonging to it. They were also to have all the books and mathematical instruments belonging to the bishop and the dean and chapter, and were authorized to set up a printing press and license books.

Cromwell died in September 1658 and his son, Richard, was memorialized by the indefatigable Grand Jury to carry out his father's intention towards his 'new erection left an orphan, scarce bound up in its swaddling clothes', so that 'by the vital beams of your piteous aspect, it may be cherished and grow'. It seemed at first to be in a fair way of doing so. There were some objections. The Quakers, predictably, opposed it as an attempt to produce a man-made ministry.[32] Oxford and Cambridge, which ought to have known better, petitioned against the proposed college as interfering with their monopoly. With the restoration of Charles II the scheme fell to pieces, and the staff scattered over England to make their mark in other places. One of them, Israel Tonge, who had been a tutor, drifted into history again as an associate of Titus Oates in the hard lying of the Popish Plot.[33]

There was no reason why the college should not have survived, in some form or other. The former prebendaries, still alive, who were coming back to claim their own from the places where they had ridden out the storm, could have carried on, if they had wished to do so. Basire, who was still in Hungary, though the university which he had served had been destroyed, petitioned Charles II to provide for him. He returned to England and his long-suffering wife in June 1661, and went on to Durham. Cosin had returned in the previous July and taken up the deanery of Peterborough, which he had been given in 1640 and lost almost as soon as he obtained it. The King intended to make him dean of Durham; but as the see was vacant, he gave him that instead, and Cosin went back to the area which he knew so well. But the bustling, self-confident young man of the twenties and thirties had grown old, and his character had hardened almost to the point of bitterness. Gifted, energetic, utterly loyal to his convictions, for sheer ability he outshone every other bishop in his day, but adversity had not taught him the grace of gentleness, and he was an easy man not to like. His driving energy, his quick temper, his certainty that he was right in everything, and therefore must overrule everyone who differed from him, made him a hard taskmaster. Baxter says that at the Savoy Conference he was as scornful of the Presbyterian position as the rest of the bishops, but his 'rustic wit and carriage' (an odd description, by the way, of a man who had spent the last eighteen years in a French court) made him easier to talk to.[34]

# 7
## THE RESTORATION

The situation, both in the cathedral and the diocese, demanded all Cosin's powers. The whole organization of the bishoprick had been destroyed, its finances were in chaos, and many of its churches in ruins. The new dean, John Barwick, was a distinguished royalist, who had been influential in bringing back the King and had refused a bishopric. He was suffering from the effects of a long and rigorous imprisonment, but he set to work at once, to bring the cathedral back to something like its old condition. Two days after his installation, on 1 November 1660, he and the six prebendaries who were available held a chapter, which resolved 'as a fruit of their thankfulness to God, to resettle the cathedral upon the ancient foundation of their statutes and laudable customs, by all prudential means and with all possible expedition'.[35]

Twenty years of neglect, robbery, and devastation had left the building hardly more than a shell. The roof was leaking, most of the windows smashed, and all the woodwork gone. There were no seats, except for a few temporary ones in the choir, which had been brought in since the Restoration. As a first step, the regular services were begun again, and a choir got together; but money had to be found for all the work that had to be done, and that was not easy. Tenants, who had been forced to buy their land during the Commonwealth or rent it from new owners, now found themselves having to take up leases from the dean and chapter, with a heavy down payment as a condition of doing so. They petitioned the King for redress of their grievances; he referred them to the commission for 'the late pretended sale of crown and church lands', who seem to have decided in the cathedral's favour about a year and a half later, though there is no record of their having done so. So the money came in. But Barwick was not to stay. St Paul's in London was in an even worse state than Durham, and he was thought to be the only man capable of dealing with it. He was succeeded, in February 1662, by John Sudbury, who carried through the work of restoration and deserves much of the credit which is so often given to Cosin.

The Bishop's part was to keep a sharp eye on everything, and urge the dean and chapter on. He officially visited the cathedral three times during the twelve years of his episcopate, putting searching questions about every aspect of its life. On the first occasion, in 1602, he wanted to know, in careful detail, whether all the proper establishment was in existence, and whether its members were doing their duty as laid down in the statutes. He was particular in his inquiries about the services, whether the petty canons attend regularly, and have clean surplices, whether they can read, and sing, skilfully? Is the precentor doing his duty, in choosing the music, in taking care of the books, and noting any absences of the dean and the prebendaries? The sacrist, who seems also to have been librarian, is asked if he has a proper catalogue, and if he is taking all the pains he can, to get back books which had been stolen during the Commonwealth?

The fabric of the church is the subject of searching inquiry. Has all the neglect of previous years been thoroughly repaired? Are they about to renew the organ, and where do they intend to put it? Have they got back Dean Hunt's altar from the people who took it away? (The altar was, in fact, retrieved and put in its old position, though the cherubs, which had adorned its front, had disappeared.) What had happened to the wood and the lead from the great broaches [spires] which had been on the Western Towers? How much money had been spent on repairs and replacements in the cathedral, and what financial provision were they making to finish the work? Had all the ancillary buildings been put in good condition and were all their muniments being properly cared for? And, finally, were all the members of the establishment behaving themselves and obeying the dean as they ought to do?[36]

The chapter replied on 12 June 1663 and endeavoured to give satisfactory answers. Up to that time they had spent £4306 3s 1d on the cathedral, and £3616 7s 3d on the repair of houses and the chancels of churches in their gift. In addition, the chapter had made the King a present of £1000, beside what had been given to him by their members as individuals. They had given £566 13s 4d to old choirmen and the poor, £400 for the redemption of captives, which, with other benefactions made a total of £13259 3s 8d. They still had to rebuild the minor canons' houses, finish the work in the choir, make a new font and pulpit, glaze four windows, repair the turrets, and mend the pavement of the church and the choir; all this, they estimated, would cost £3000.[37] It is clear from their answers that there were not yet as many services as there used to be and that the prebendal houses were in bad shape.

It was a considerable accomplishment, but the Bishop was not satisfied and in two further visitations, in 1665 and in 1668, he probed more deeply into what had been done and left undone. There was a difficulty in getting minor canons, and the Bishop comments that they would get them if they paid them more; if they do not fill up the number, the King shall know of it. They ought to have a proper schoolmaster, instead of a probationer. What they say about sackbuts and cornets (probably in connection with the inquiry about organs) had nothing to do with the case, but the Bishop will allow them because they were in use in his time. Though no mention is made of it, a little organ had been bought in London for £80 and set up in a loft, on the South Side of the choir, in June-July 1661. Before Dean Barwick left, he had given an order for a great organ, which was first used on Christmas Day 1662. The Bishop, who had obviously been looking round, complained that the music books were torn and both the altar and the choir meanly furnished, and that some of the needed repairs had either not been done, or badly done.

The prebendaries, he says, are not doing their duty, and they have not mentioned that they come into the choir in nightgowns [dressing gowns] and grey stockings, or of wearing 'long rapiers, great skirted jumps [loose coats], and short daggers'. The Dean himself receives some criticism. No doubt the nice things the chapter say about him are true, but there was no need for him to have signed them himself. That he attends more services than his duty requires is commendable, but has nothing to do with the Bishop's questions. His claim that he has not taken advantage of all the absences allowed him does not square with his being away all the previous June.

Much of it had the air of fault-finding for its own sake, and the chapter obviously felt that they were being hardly dealt with. It is easy to find excuses for their, occasionally, unusual dress. The half-ruined cathedral must have been cold enough to justify the dressing gowns at the early morning service, and most of them had worn lay clothes during the Commonwealth, and might from time to time drop back into the habit. Cosin, however, confirmed their ancient privileges; these included the right not to be visited officially by anybody but their own bishop, and the charge of the spiritualities during a vacancy in the see.

Sudbury and his colleagues were dealing manfully with their difficulties. Some of the work which they put in is still among the glories of the cathedral, particularly the carving of the choir stalls and the cover of the font, with their mixed gothic, and renaissance designs. The architect is said to have been James Clement, who died in 1690. There must have been a flourishing school of woodworkers at the time in Durham, for their skill is apparent not only here, but also at Brancepeth and Sedgefield churches, in which Cosin was personally interested. The new men, who were brought in to fill the vacant stalls, were all in their way outstanding. Among them was Daniel Brevint, whom Cosin had presented for ordination in the Embassy Chapel in Paris during his stay there. He was afterwards the author of *The Christian Sacrament and Sacrifice*, a eucharistic manual much used by the early Methodists. William Sancroft, afterwards archbishop of Canterbury, exchanged a stall at Westminster for one at Durham. John Durel, also ordained in Paris, translated the Prayer Book into French for the benefit of the Channel Islanders. Thomas Wood, afterwards bishop of Lichfield, was appointed by the King, much against the will of Cosin, who by no means approved of either his character or his theology.

The most vivid personality among the new-comers was Dennis Granville who, for the next twenty-six years was to enliven the life of the cathedral very considerably.[38] He belonged to the great West Country family of Granville (or Grenville) and was brother to the Earl of Bath. In 1660 he married Cosin's daughter Anne, a feeble-minded girl who later on was rather given to drink. Related to a bishop and an earl and with some influence at court, Granville was not likely to go without preferment. His father-in-law made him archdeacon of Durham and prebendary of the First Stall and presented him with the rectories of Easington and Elwick, the latter of which he exchanged for the more desirable living of Sedgefield. Cosin made no secret of the fact that he had given Granville all this partly as a financial provision for him and partly to please Lord Bath. There was no doubt about the sincerity of Granville's religion and his desire to do well, but defects of character, including an enormous capacity for getting into debt, ruined many of his good intentions. His money troubles led to lifelong difficulties, including the greatest humiliation that he ever had to suffer. On 8 July 1674, as he was passing through the cloisters after a funeral which had been attended by the leading people of the county, bailiffs arrested him for debt. They took no notice of his claim that as one of the King's chaplains, he could not be taken into such custody, and the Under-Sheriff refused to interfere. He was put into gaol 'with many aggravating circumstances'. Granville appealed to the King, who ordered both the Under-Sheriff and the creditor, who had caused the arrest, to be prosecuted; but they were forgiven, on their submission and their explanation of their conduct that they did not know Mr Granville to be a King's chaplain. He plagued his father-in-law continually to pay over Anne's dowry, which Cosin refused to do, feeling pretty sure that if he did, it would be swallowed up by Granville's creditors; and a nagging correspondence went on between them, which made Granville think himself very ill-used.

Cosin died in January 1672. Age, opposition, and the continual pain of the stone had made him even more difficult. His disappointing son John, who had become a Roman Catholic, said that he would 'rather trail a pike for his bread' than live at home with his father; and did so, in the King's guards.[39] Cosin had alienated most of the influential people of the bishoprick by refusing to allow them to send representatives to parliament, which would have injured the independent status of the principality; that, and his over-heavy hand in all his affairs, had not left him many friends. Isaac Basire, one of the dwindling number of those who remembered his early days, preached his funeral sermon, dwelling on his generosity, which had been lavish, and his eminent services both to Church and State.[40]

# 8
## WAYS OF PREFERMENT

The see remained vacant and the Duke of Monmouth is said to have received the revenues until, sometimes in 1673, Nathaniel Crewe, the bishop of Oxford, was advised by his father to ask for translation to Durham. He obtained the promise of it, but somehow could make no further progress, until Lord Lumley told him that the king had promised Nell Gwyn a payment out of the appointment; until she got her money nothing would be done. Through an agent, Crewe arranged to give her £5000 or £6000, and there was no further trouble.[41] He was enthroned on 10 November 1674. For the last ten years of his life Dean Sudbury worked under the eye of a less censorious bishop. By 1683 the ornate screen of carved oak, which was to stand at the entrance to the choir, replacing the ancient stone one, which had been destroyed, must have been complete or nearly so, for in that year Sudbury made an agreement with Bernard Smith, the famous Father Smith, to build a great organ to stand on the screen, though it was not finished until three years after Sudbury's death. The other major work which he began, but left

63

uncompleted, was the building of the library.

In monastic days, the greater part of the books had been kept in various places, where they were handiest for the people who were to use them. The general reserve was in a room over the slype, which is now the song school. Since the service books were all destroyed, we do not know what was the use of Durham, but the library escaped fairly well. All the volumes were brought together in the room over the slype and in 1628 the chapter repaired the building, made new shelves, and 'newly composed those ancient manuscripts and other books, whereof the inequity of former times had not yet made a full spoil, to be the better preserved hereafter'. To provide funds for the library, the dean was to pay 26 marks on his installation, and every prebendary 20 nobles; and a tenth of every sum involved, was to be paid whenever a lease or a patent was sealed. When persons other than members of the corporate body or their families wished to be buried in the church or choir, they were to pay 40 shillings to the library.[42] Larger premises were now needed. The old frater house had become the petty canons' hall, but like much else had fallen into ruin during the Commonwealth. Sudbury began to rebuild it and fit it out as a library at his own expense. He had already spent over £1000 on it when, feeling that he might never live to see it finished, he made his will on 11 January 1683 and ordered his executors to pay out whatever sums were needed to complete the library, according to the specifications he had laid down.

Everybody knew that the Dean's health was failing, and manoeuvering began for so important a piece of preferment. Granville was in London, in attendance at court, and well placed to look after his interests. Crewe, the bishop of Durham, was anxious to get the deanery for his nephew, Dr Montague, the fourth son of the Earl of Sandwich, to whom he had already given the lucrative mastership of Sherburn Hospital, and was willing to do a little trading on his behalf. If Granville would give up trying to get the deanery and support Montague, he would see that he got the mastership of Sherburn, which he would persuade Montague to resign. In a disingenuous letter to Sir Richard Lloyd, who was expected to act as a go-between, the Bishop lists all the advantages of Sherburn over the deanery. It was the sort of post which could be held with all the other preferment which Granville already had. It carried a great deal of patronage. It was practically a sinecure, for the manager of the hospital would do all the work and pay the master £340 a year. With an eye, no doubt, to Granville's frequent financial embarrassments, he added, as a subtle touch, that Sherburn would offer 'a place of retirement upon occasions'. On the other hand, the deanery was only worth £1300 a year, and entailed a great deal of expenditure. Granville would probably have to give up his other preferment and would lose on the exchange. Instead of being the sole authority, as he would be at Sherburn, he would have to work with the chapter, who could be very troublesome now and then.

If Lloyd passed all this on to Granville he was not impressed. Indeed he might very well wonder why, if Sherburn was so desirable, Montague wanted to leave it. Meanwhile, he was on the spot, and had friends at court, particularly a Lady B, who could speak to the King at the right moment. He does not say who Lady B is, but possibly he means Lady Bath. Archbishop Sancroft was strongly against the appointment. He had been a colleague of Granville's at Durham for a short time and did not think him 'worthy of the least stall there'. In spite of Granville's efforts, he would not change his mind, but Crewe, realizing that his nephew stood no chance, swung round and supported Granville, telling Sancroft, who remonstrated with him about it, that 'he would rather choose a gentleman than a silly fellow who knew nothing but books'. To which the Archbishop replied, 'I beshrew thee!'[43] Court influence was enough, and Charles II good-naturedly promised that Granville should not only have the deanery, but should keep the archdeaconry and all his other preferment as well.

In a jubilant paper, written for his own satisfaction, Granville detailed 'all the happy acts of God's providence towards the Archdeacon of Durham'; including the fact that he had a cough and a bad leg, which kept him in London at the essential time; that his brother, the Earl of Bath, had been inspired to write to the King at a seasonable moment; and that Lady B had been able to exert her influence.[44] Unlike most of his colleagues on the chapter, Granville was no scholar. He had been created master of arts at Oxford on 28 September 1660, 'by favour of his great relations', without going through the usual exercises; a proceeding which annoyed Anthony Wood, who thought such a grace should be reserved for those who had suffered in the King's cause.

Though not overburdened with intelligence, Granville was guided by a few fixed ideas, which were good enough in themselves. One was the absolute necessity of a strict adherence to the rubrics of the Book of Common Prayer, and he drew up a paper in which he detailed seven points in which they were disobeyed. The chief was that they had only a monthly sacrament, when the Prayer Book laid down that it should be celebrated weekly. To this, he added a further seven 'omissions and irregularities'. There was no sermon on Ash Wednesday, Good Friday, or Wednesdays and Fridays in Lent and Advent as there used to be. There was slackness on the part of servants in attending the six o'clock prayers, particularly on Sundays and Holy Days. Surplices were often so 'nasty and dirty', that they gave 'much offence to people'. There was also the rather extraordinary 'behaviour of some petty canons, in sitting on their desks, with their backsides towards the choir'. 'Irregularities within the verge of the cathedral' ran to twenty-seven items; including the wearing of 'boisterous perriwigs' with surplices; choir boys badgering people for money and thrusting books on people who did not want them; dogs being allowed to go into the choir; and beggars standing at the choir door; as well as people punching one another as they tried to get near to the preacher. Cattle were being fed in the churchyard and linen was dried there. It gives a picture of a place that was certainly alive, if not overdecorous.[45]

A weekly Celebration was Granville's ideal, and he strove hard to attain it both in the parish churches in his care, and in the cathedral. When his colleagues of the chapter were reluctant to fall in with his plans, he wrote to the Archbishop of Canterbury to bring pressure to bear and see that they came into line. The objections seem to have been that it was an innovation to have a weekly Celebration, and that the long preparation for receiving the sacrament, which was demanded by the devotional practice of the time, would be burdensome if it had to be carried out once a week. But he got his way in the end and set to work to persuade other cathedrals to do the same. Possibly because of more frequent Celebrations, sometime between 1686 and 1689, when Robert Delavel was mayor of Durham, the chapter decided to have their altar plate remade; and Granville gave a receipt to Delavel, for 'one bason, two candlesticks, two flagons, two chalices and two pattens of gilt plate' belonging to the Bishop, to be lent by him for the use of the cathedral, while its own vessels were being 'changed'. These were to be returned to Robert Delavel, or such a person as the Bishop should appoint, upon demand 'safe whole and in as good condition as when it was received'.[46]

Granville was anxious about the training of his curates and the minor canons. He wished to encourage their studies with regular lectures and ultimately to reward the deserving among them with chapter livings. He seems to have given as much oversight and

6 Nave, and choir screen destroyed by Salvin. Drawn 1841 by R. G. Billings

7 Nave today with Scott's screen and pulpit

9 Bishop Hatfield's tomb and the episcopal throne

8 Scott's high altar enclosing Dean Hunt's marble altar

personal attention to his parishes as could be expected from a man with so much preferment, insisting on strict discipline for others, though he was not always capable of imposing it on himself, in spite of much self-examination, and many resolutions to amend. He was a copious and often entertaining letter-writer, displaying his own naivety, and his passion for laying down rules for other people's conduct on every occasion. He was a likeable man in the main, though his friends must often have found him wildly exasperating. In spite of his unhappy marriage and his habit of getting mixed up in more quarrels than he ought to have done, he would have done very well, if only he could have escaped from the morass of his debts. When these were particularly pressing, he would have a fit of repentance about them and try to make a fresh start, only to succeed in getting more involved than ever. With an income from all his offices of £2308 13s 2d, a very large sum in modern money, he should have been able to manage; but for years he had borrowed from everybody who would lend him anything, and his debts had been so exchanged and traded about that it was beyond his power to disentangle them.[47] In extenuation of his quarrels, it may be said that these were probably hard to avoid in an age when most people drank too much and were therefore quick to take offence.

# 9
# THE EXILE AND HIS STEWARD

James II's flight from England in 1688 brought the Dean's affairs to a crisis. He believed firmly that the Church of England was irrevocably committed to the doctrine of the Divine Right of Kings and non-resistance under any provocation, a conviction which was reinforced by his sense of personal obligation to the House of Stuart. In his opinion rebellion was the worst of sins. All the talk of conscience was too reminiscent of what had happened in 1640 and would lead to the same result. The Church of England was in no danger and if she was, she must submit to it and suffer in silence. He made a strong attempt to convince the cathedral clergy and the local gentry of the rightness of these opinions, but with no success.

On 5 December 1688 Lord Lumley entered Durham with fifty horsemen, accompanied by gentry from Durham and Yorkshire, and declared for the Prince of Orange. Captain Ireton with ten troopers was sent to seize the Dean's horses and order him to be confined to his house during Lord Lumley's stay in the city. It seemed to the

Dean that Durham was now a dangerous place; he therefore resolved to go to Carlisle, where the governor, a Roman Catholic, was still loyal to James. However, William's supporters took over there also and Granville left for Scotland, but he was arrested and plundered on the way. After he had been taken back to Carlisle, his money was returned to him and he was told to go home to Durham, but he stayed on for another fortnight and preached in the cathedral to convince the public that, in spite of their suspicions, he was no Roman Catholic. Then he went on to Edinburgh, and from there to France where, apart from one short visit to England, made incognito in 1695 to raise a little money, he stayed for the rest of his life.[48] On his stubborn refusal to take the oath of allegiance to William and Mary, which made it impossible for him to stay in England, his friend, Dr Thomas Comber, the precentor of York, was given the deanery from which he had fled; though he insisted to the end that the office was still his and that he could only regard Comber as his steward, who would have to give a strict account of all the money he had received when James came into his own again. Meanwhile he lived quietly in France, where his stubborn Anglicanism did not make him very welcome to the exiled court. On the death of Archbishop Lamplugh, James made him the titular archbishop of York, but otherwise he was neglected. He died on 18 April 1703 in debt, of course, but optimistic to the last.

Comber was as devoted to the Book of Common Prayer as ever Granville was and had written long and learned expositions of it, which still have their value; but he was also strongly critical of the Church of Rome and had continued Thomas Traherne's exposure of *Roman Forgeries*, as well as being a busy pamphleteer on behalf of William and Mary. He found the deanery almost ruinous, a condition which is mentioned again and again, due no doubt to the fact that most deans having other preferment, chose to live elsewhere, except for short periods of official residence. Most of the prebendal houses were also in a bad state; that belonging to Dr Brevint of the Tenth Stall, collapsed entirely during a storm in December 1674, though no one was hurt. The patching up which they had received in the first years after the Restoration to make them habitable was not enough; and most of them were improved or partly rebuilt in the last years of the seventeenth or the first years of the eighteenth century. The cathedral was now in better shape, and attention could be given to the bells, which Comber caused to be recast in London in June 1693. The work, costing £300, was paid for by subscription,

Comber giving a good deal of the money himself. Bishop Crewe refused to contribute.

Comber was very active in many other ways as well. He began afforestation on waste land belonging to the cathedral at Bear Park and completely renovated the water supply of the college (as the close at Durham is always called), which was distributed to the different houses through an octagonal stone tower, still standing, at the West End of the green, and which he largely rebuilt. Again Bishop Crewe refused to give a penny and came in for some sharp words from the Dean for his niggardliness. The Bishop's revenues are large, says Comber, implying that there should be an equally large generosity, and the Bishop's cattle would benefit from the new water supply, which meant that there was an obligation to help pay for it. A later chapter minute refers to a pool at the foot of the water tower for the use of cattle, and it was no doubt this to which Comber was referring. There is a Durham tradition that in the drought of the following summer, the Bishop sent to borrow water from the chapter and was told that he could not have any.

An attempt to mine coal at Bear Park proved unsuccessful. There was no sale for it, and when the man in charge died, Comber abandoned the pit with a loss of £60. He had better luck with his efforts to get back lands at Croxdale and Stainforth belonging to the dean and chapter; the tenants admitted in the end that their claim to own them was false and that they were only leasehold. Church property was particularly open to encroachment and there were some cases which could only be settled in the law courts. A useful piece of work was to replace the old wooden bridge, which formed an exit from the Peninsula at the South End, and which needed continual repair, by a stone structure, the abutments of which can still be seen about a hundred yards above the present bridge.

The chapter had other responsibilities, which they did not forget. In accordance with their statutes they had always maintained a public school; now, in response perhaps to the growing movement for charity schools, they joined with the Justices of the Peace, and the Bishop of Durham, in providing a schoolmaster, at £40 a year, to teach fourteen poor girls reading, and spinning. The girls were to be kept at school for a year, and then sent home, equipped to get their own living and another fourteen taken in their place. But 'several ill-disposed persons' ruined the scheme. The new library made 'a very handsome appearance', and the chapter was prepared to spend money on equipping it properly; buying, among other books, 'a complete edition of all the classics, with notes' and having a proper catalogue made. The fine collection, now in the old refectory, was built up during the next hundred years. Comber had always been friendly with Dr George Hickes, the greatest scholar among the Non-jurors, and he now persuaded the chapter to give £20 towards the publication of Hickes' *Anglo-Saxon Grammar*, a pioneering work of scholarship. They also gave £20 to buy books for the clergy who were going to America with Dr Bray to convert the Indians. With all the ordinary routine of cathedral life, his chaplaincy to the Queen, and much preaching and writing, Comber's eight years as dean were well filled with work. His death on 25 November 1699, came at the end of a long series of disturbances in Church and State. But these were now over. A cardinal point in the Reformation struggle had been finally decided. The monarch was not to be a Roman Catholic.[49]

# 3

# *The Eighteenth Century and After*

---

## 1

## RATIONALISM AND HIGH LIVING

After Comber's death, John Montague, Bishop Crewe's nephew, got the deanery at last, and spent an unremarkable twenty-nine years in its occupancy. He was succeeded by Dr Henry Bland, a name which was to appear with some frequency in the subsequent history of Durham. He had been a fellow student and friend of Walpole and was first master and then provost of Eton during his time as dean. With many of its best men lost to the Non-jurors and suspect for their attachment to the house of Stuart, the Established Church settled down to a complacent materialism. By the middle of the eighteenth century the majority of educated people had either repudiated Christianity openly or come to disregard it entirely in their lives. The various brands of reduced Christianity, which sprang up in this atmosphere, could do nothing to improve the situation. A deeper rather than a more accommodating presentation of the faith was needed. This was provided on the intellectual side by Joseph Butler, a Durham clergyman, whose famous *Analogy* appeared in 1736, and by the work of Wesley and Whitefield which brought a new fervour to religious life; thus slowly the tide was made to turn. But for a long time a secular and rationalistic spirit filled the Church and stifled its life. Any moderately well paid post in the establishment was regarded simply as property, to be acquired as eagerly as any other, with little restraining sense of the responsibility for souls which went with it. Most clergy felt no deeper spiritual commitment than the average well-meaning layman. Work in the parishes was done by curates, who were often without education and always without powerful friends. Places worth having were taken by the offshoots of great families, who, disinclined for the armed forces or the law, yet needing money to supplement a younger son's allowance, took Orders with the prospect of a rich benefice. Others were men

71

who had accompanied some young nobleman round Europe, and were rewarded by political influence being exerted on their behalf. Only a few tough thrusting personalities managed to attract enough notice to make it difficult for them to be overlooked.

In the early years of the eighteenth century, there was a group of men at Durham, each of some distinction, and each in his own way indicative of his time. Thomas Rundle (1688?–1743) as a young man at Oxford was the close friend of Edward Talbot, son of the bishop of Salisbury. Rundle had a taste for fashionable life and advanced thinking. For a time he was intimate with Whiston and Chubb, and got a reputation for being a Deist. Unguarded remarks made at this time were remembered against him. London life had also brought him in touch with the literary circles of his day, and Swift was his friend. Though Edward Talbot died, the Bishop continued to take an interest in Rundle and after his ordination, gave him considerable preferment in the Salisbury diocese. When Talbot went to Durham in 1721, he presented Rundle to a stall in the cathedral and had him to live with him as a personal friend and chaplain at Auckland Castle. He also gave him a good deal more, including the living of Sedgefield and the usual plum of the diocese, the mastership of Sherburn Hospital. Charles Talbot, the Bishop's son, became Lord Chancellor of England and put his friend Rundle forward for the bishopric of Gloucester. The nomination had already been made public, but Gibson, the bishop of London, opposed it strongly and prevented the appointment being completed. Though Rundle insisted that he was no Deist, and had, indeed, preached against the Deists' doctrines, enough suspicion of him remained to make him unacceptable. The Lord Chancellor felt himself snubbed, but succeeded, a little later, in getting Rundle the far richer diocese of Londonderry. For the rest of his life he lived mainly in Dublin and, though he had a reputation for being generous, left a large fortune behind him when he died. He is said to have permanently ruined his health by high living while at Durham.[1]

Probably to soothe the Lord Chancellor for the rebuff he had suffered, Gloucester was given to another protégé of his, Martin Benson (1689–1752), also a prebendary of Durham, whose goodness was revered by everybody. Though Gloucester was one of the poorest sees, he announced his intention of never exchanging it for another, though he kept his stall at Durham and some other preferment.

Joseph Spence (1699–1768) was one of those fortunate people who make friends easily and among all classes.[2] Everybody who met him liked him and wanted more of his acquaintance. A parson's son, with some help from a patron in the beginning, he made his way from Winchester to a fellowship at New College, Oxford. That university made him professor of poetry, and paid him the compliment of extending the appointment for another term. Afterwards he was given the sinecure post of professor of history. A critical essay on Pope's translation of the Odyssey brought him the friendship of the poet, and intimacy with the most outstanding literary personalities of the time. Dr Johnson, in his magisterial way, pronounced Spence to be a man 'whose learning was not very great and whose mind was not very powerful',[3] though he admitted that the criticism of Pope, as far as it went, was sound enough. Other works, including a study of classical mythology called *Polymetis* enhanced Spence's reputation. He made three visits to the Continent with rich young men in his charge; one of them was a relative of Bishop Trevor, who in May 1754 gave him a stall at Durham. His friend, Lord Lincoln, had presented him with a house at Byfleet in Surrey, where he had developed a well-known garden, and for the rest of his life he divided his time between Byfleet and Durham. He was the friend and patron of Stephen Duck, the thresher poet, who got himself ordained and became rector of Byfleet. Robert Dodsley, who had started life as a footman, but turned author, playwright, and bookseller, owed much to Spence at the start of his career, and the two were close friends for life. It was to Spence's house in Durham that Dodsley came in his last illness, hoping that a change of air and rest in the country would give him a few more years to live, but it did not. He died there, and was buried in the cathedral churchyard, beneath a flat brown stone with an elaborate epitaph, which was probably written by Spence.[4] He had been a leading publisher in his day, the friend of Johnson, and the initiator of the famous *Dictionary*. All the wits had met at his shop and Spence had known them all, but it was his association with Pope which gave him his chief importance. A collection of anecdotes, which he left unpublished at his death, throws great light on many of the personalities of his day, and is indispensable for a right appreciation of Pope.

Another of the Durham prebendaries, a man of a different type, also built a large part of his fame on his intimacy with Pope. William Warburton (1698–1779), a large-boned robust man, was the son of the town clerk of Newark, and himself practised as an attorney for a while. Taking Orders, he obtained a country living, and passed his time in voracious reading. Soon he began to publish, and came to know many of the minor authors of the time. He is not a very amiable character. As often as not, he began by abusing the people whom later on he found it in his interest to cultivate. He was at first very critical of the *Essay on Man*, and then put Pope in his debt by strongly defending it against attacks on its inadequate philosophy.[5] He was a voluminous author, his best book being one on Church and State, the most talked of being *The Divine Legation of Moses*, an attempt to prove that the absence of any reference to a future life in the Old Testament was an indication of its divine origin. Dogmatic, arrogant, delighting in controversy, in which it was said that he wrangled rather than reasoned, he was not a man to let himself be overlooked. In 1755 he was given a stall at Durham, and two years later added the deanery of Bristol to his collection of preferment. A Durham tradition says that when in a bad temper one day, he refused to wear a cope, as it interfered with his full-bottomed wig, and that his refusal led to the wearing of copes being discontinued there. In 1759 he was made bishop of Gloucester. Pope and the diocese of Gloucester were very prominent at Durham in those days. He remained a prebendary of Durham until his death at the age of 81.

From 1746 to 1774, a period which includes all those just mentioned except Rundle, Spencer Cowper was the dean.[6] He took orders reluctantly, as the only means of providing for a younger son of his temperament who had the certainty of royal favour and strong family influence. While he was waiting for something really good, his family obtained for him the living of Fordwich in Kent and a prebend at Canterbury. All the time that he was at Durham, his heart was in his native Hertfordshire, to which he hurried back as soon as his official residence was over. The long correspondence, which he kept up with his brother, Earl Cowper, and other relatives, gives us a clear, and, on the whole, an attractive picture of him. He had bad eyesight and worried continually about his own and his wife's health. His letters are full of their ailments and the appalling remedies they took for them. There is gossip about the prebendaries, such as Dr Leslie, who became bishop of Limerick, and tied up the weathercock to make sure that the wind would be right for him to go over there. The same person, in reply to an inquiry about his wife, after the birth of a child, replied: 'We are as well as can be expected.' Martin Benson was the colleague whom he found most congenial. Spence and he probably rarely met, as their residence was at different times.

Music was Spencer Cowper's chief interest, and during his time in Durham, which was usually from September to the end of November, he was the moving spirit in a music society there, and also liked to have the choirmen in to sing to him from time to time. Much of the great collection of eighteenth-century music now in the library, was got together by him. He appreciated the beauty of the river banks and of the surrounding countryside, but disliked the city intensely. It was still a medieval town, the narrow streets of which were blocked by the gates of the ancient citadel. The deanery, when he arrived, was in 'a sad rugged rough condition'. The late dean had kept it 'wind and water tight' but nothing more.[7] The furniture, for which he was charged £260, 'would not sell for as many shillings in Moorfields, for nobody would buy it'. He found the cathedral unattractive, being filled with 'massy pillars out of all proportion'. He approved of the choir because it was like a college chapel and there was 'a very fine organ, a good organist, and tolerable voices'. When he arrived, the medieval copes were still worn, and he would have liked to get rid of them, as 'mere frippery and scandalous', but he thought that his brethren were 'so attached to their finery' that they would never agree. Warburton proved him wrong in that respect. Durham itself he never liked; to him it was 'a rough dirty place', through which nothing passed but 'Scotch peers, Scotch members, and Scotch pedlars'.[8] He had an equally low opinion of most of the local squires, many of whom he thought uncouth, and some even gross. He wanted no more of their society than was unavoidable. He was on neighbourly terms with the bishops who passed through the see in his time, without being very enthusiastic about any of them. Joseph Butler, who was translated from Bristol, was in Durham too short a time to make much impact, (October 1750 to June 1752) and, though he delivered one important charge in the cathedral, his great work as a philosopher was already done. Bishop Trevor, who succeeded him, the dean treats with good humoured tolerance. He was a large eater, who tried to work off the inevitable fat with violent exercise, a stupid proceeding in both its parts in Cowper's opinion.

Heavy eating and drinking were a prominent feature in the lives of the prebendaries. The statutes enjoined that when one of them was in residence, he should keep 'more sumptuous entertainment' than at other times in the year, 'giving meat to the choir and inviting citizens and strangers'.[9] This had now grown into a series of feasts, given to the mayor and corporation, the local gentry, the clergy, the bedesmen, and others in turn. A cook had been provided for originally to serve the common table which had been kept in the petty canons' hall; but now that was no longer in use, he went to whichever prebendary happened to be in residence. Spencer Cowper, naturally an abstemious man, loathed all this perpetual gorging. For three quarters of the year chapter business was done in his absence, and the documents which needed his signature were sent to him in Hertfordshire. But when he was in residence he did his duty according to his lights. He preached a few conventional sermons and complained that the congregation would clatter up out of the nave, to gather round the pulpit in the choir, an ornate two-decker with panels depicting saints, with a heavy sounding board above it, which had been put there in 1726 at the cost of £196 16s. Some of these sermons he published, as a dignitary should, together with a letter to a niece on her first receiving the Blessed Sacrament. Spencer Cowper's letters show a sensitive, often humorous, tolerant man, who would have been perfectly happy to live somewhere near London, and occupy his time with cultured pursuits rather than be a dean; but he needed money, and the Church offered him the least unpleasant way of getting it. Disliking Durham as he did, it would have seemed to him ironic that he should die there, but it would have pleased him that at his burial in the Nine Altars, the music was that of Croft and Purcell.[10]

The choir always had a good deal of attention from the chapter. Heseltine, the organist, had a salary of £100 a year, and when his post was vacant, it was much sought after. The singing men were paid sums varying from £20 to £40 a year and were recruited from all over England. Spencer Cowper once congratulated himself that he had got a man from Winchester who was 'one of the best voices he had ever heard'. A good deal of money was spent on seeing that they were properly trained; one of them was even sent to London for a special course. Prayers were still held at six o'clock in the morning for the college servants and the choirmen were frequently admonished for not attending. The boys were taught and clothed in return for their services, and when their voices broke, the chapter paid to have them apprenticed.

The ongoing life of the cathedral is reflected in the chapter minutes. Between 1727 and 1730 they began to repave the choir and the nave, thus making good the last of the destruction during the Commonwealth. Something seems to have held up the work, for three years later it was still not fully completed.[11] The Nine Altars had been used as a timber store, but in 1752 the chapter ordered that a shed should be built for that purpose, and the chapel cleaned and put into a decent condition.[12] The canons' desks in the choir were raised, and something was to be done about the draughts. New furniture was provided for the communion table, pulpit and stalls; this was probably the scarlet hangings, which were there for the rest of the century. The consistory court had been in the Galilee since Cardinal Langley's time; and now the registrar was allowed to enclose an office there, and another for his clerk, as well as to make a repository for wills. The great flood of 1770, which ruined much of the Tyne Valley, and raised the level of the river Wear in Durham, eight feet ten inches higher than any previous record, swept away Dean Comber's bridge, and the chapter replaced it with the present Prebends' Bridge, a hundred yards or so to the west of the previous site. Its architect was a local man, Mr George Nicholson. The old bridge had only been wide enough to take a man on horseback; its parapet was so low that one dark night a gentleman returning home with a group of companions, disappeared over it, horse and all, and his friends never knew that he had gone until they reached their journey's end. Now it was made wide enough to take 'gentlemen's carriages, which the chapter allow to pass over without toll'.[13]

2

# THE FABRIC IN GREAT DECAY

The increasing prosperity of the North East had greatly enriched some of the chapter lands, so that their holders were known as the Golden Canons. The common fund was distributed yearly, when at this time the dean received from it on an average £40 and each of the prebendaries a little over £33, as an addition to the income from their separate estates. The proceeds of the chapter woods, mines, and quarries were still devoted to the fabric fund, but that source proved insufficient for the work that had to be done, and money had to be found by other means. It was obvious that the church building was in a bad state, and in 1777 the chapter asked Mr John Wooler, a local architect, to make a thorough survey. He sent in his report on 29 November, only a few days after he had been approached, and it was very alarming.[14] There was a crack running along the vaulting on the South Side of the nave from the entrance to the choir to the line of marble in the floor at the West End. Neither he nor his assistants, Mr Gibbons and Mr Nicholson, had noticed it before, though on close examination it looked to be of long standing. The wall of the South Aisle, towards the cloister, was bulging, and both these faults he attributed to the original builders, because they did not put in buttresses and tie beams. He recommended that the crack should be filled with plaster and closely watched.

The four turrets on the North and South Ends of the Nine Altars, the two turrets at the North End of the crossing, and the two buttresses at the East End of it were in such a bad state that they would have to be taken down and entirely rebuilt. He had noticed and 'indeed it is obvious to everybody' that the stone-work on the outside of the whole building was heavily eroded, so that water was lying in the stones and seeping into the building. He recommended, as the cheapest way of dealing with this problem, that the surface should be chipped away to the depth of one, two, or three, inches, the worst stones replaced, and the whole repointed. Until then the cathedral had no down-comers, so he suggested that while the scaffolding was up, lead pipes should be fitted to carry off the water from the roof. The mullions and side-jambs of the windows would have to be renewed; they were so bad as scarcely to hold the glass. The parapets on the top of the building, as well as the corbels supporting the low wall round the bell-ringers' gallery in the great tower, had many defects, and needed to be renewed. 'The long buttresses which support the angles of the tower' were in poor condition, particularly near the top. The upper part of the porch, on the North Side of the cathedral, had pulled away from the wall, and needed to be taken down and finished at a lower pitch. There were some 'trifling faults' in the foundations of the Galilee but they could be put right. As additional improvements, in case the chapter wished to make them, he suggested that 'four larger and four smaller ragged pinnacles of stone' should be placed at the corners, and in the middle of each of the four sides of the top of the great tower, and similarly on the top of the two western towers, with open parapets. As the western towers were never used, he proposed that the windows should be filled up, with 'the blackest flint stone' leaving small apertures for a circulation of air. This, he thought, would greatly relieve the 'massy appearance of the whole structure'. The men of the eighteenth century had no sympathy for the vast strength of the building, which has seemed so impressive to multitudes since. The pinnacles he recommended were put on at a later date, but though some of the lower windows were blocked with stone, the 'blackest flint stone' that he wanted was never used.

It was a daunting list of things to be done, and his method of calculating the expense of it all is interesting. He thought that the work would need twenty-four masons, with sixteen labourers to attend them, and two carts with two horses each, to bring the materials. Leaving out Sundays, and the two winter months, they could work 250 days in the year. At 2s a day, 'which is considerably above the mark', the forty men would cost £1000 a year; the carts at 5s a day each, would come to £125 a year. The work on the Nine Altars would take two years, the rest another six years, at a total cost of £9000. Though he did not mention it, he obviously expected the stone to come from the cathedral's own quarries and the men who built it would also cut it. The chipping of the exterior, which ruined much of the original decoration, and the destruction of the porch above the North Door, is generally quoted to Wyatt's discredit, but it is clear that Wooler suggested it seventeen years before Wyatt had anything to do with the building.

What was done about the crack and the bulging wall is not clear. Probably it was patched up for a time, as the exterior of the South Wall, which had fallen away, was not rebuilt until the 1840s. In February 1779 Wooler supplied detailed instructions to the master mason for work on the pinnacles.[15] He was obviously the consultant and Nicholson the supervisor on the spot. Early prints show what were really turrets on the North Side of the Nine Altars, one broken off at the roof line; these Wooler replaced by small spires. He proposed to use a good many iron clamps which, he said, could be prevented from rusting if they were first heated, then dipped in linseed oil, and afterwards given three coats of white-lead. They did indeed last until 1961 when they finally corroded, and split the stone so that the pinnacles had to be rebuilt. The South End of the Nine Altars with its turrets was restored by Ignatius Bonomi in 1826–8. From the latter half of the eighteenth to the latter half of the nineteenth century, some major work or other was always on hand in the cathedral. Architects came and went with their ideas being interpreted, and often changed, by the clerk of works who carried them out. The main impress on the cathedral as it is today is that of Anthony Salvin and Sir George Gilbert Scott.

But before they appeared another influence had been at work. On 26 September 1794, the chapter agreed that 'Mr James Wyatt be wrote to, to come down and inspect the repairs of the cathedral, and to give a plan for further repairs and improvements'. Mr Wyatt came down and was full of ideas. He pronounced the chapter house to be ruinous, though many others strongly disagreed with him. However, the chapter felt that the man from London must be right and ordered Mr Morpeth, their clerk of works, to pull it down; which he did by taking out the keystone, so that the roof of the Eastern End fell in of its own weight.[16] The Dean afterwards said that he disagreed with the proceeding, though he was present at the meeting which gave the order. A comfortable vestry for the prebendaries was made out of the bit of the building which was left. Wyatt had further plans. He proposed to bring the floor of the Nine Altars up to the level of the rest of the church, to carry the choir through at its present level to the East Wall of the Nine Altars, and in the space thus created to erect a baldachin over the altar, out of the materials of the Neville Screen and Bishop Hatfield's tomb. His suggestion was not accepted. An even more ambitious plan was to pull down the Galilee Chapel, and in its place make a carriage drive up to the great West Door of the cathedral, which had been blocked for so long by Langley's tomb. In preparation for this, the consistory court was moved into the North Transept, and the registry into the dormitory. The improvers had got as far as taking off the roof of the Galilee, when a public outcry frightened Dean Cornwallis and the idea was abandoned.

The idea of destroying the Galilee could well be dropped, but the roof of the cathedral urgently needed attention, and on Wyatt's advice the lead was stripped off and sold and replaced with slates. This and other work was done under the eye of Mr Morpeth, the clerk of the works, who had a very free hand in what he did. The resident architect was Mr George Nicholson, who seems to have had the task of working out the general ideas of the consultant. As Nicholson was on the spot, he came in for most of the blame from those who were critical of what was being done. Much of what was characteristic of the external appearance of the cathedral disappeared; among other things, a half-obliterated effigy of a milkmaid and her cow, on the West Turret at the North End of the Nine Altars, which was supposed to represent the woman who guided the monks with St Cuthbert's coffin to the Dunholm, but which more probably indicated that the cathedral's wealth came from its rich farm lands. This Nicholson replaced with a couple of eighteenth-century dairy maids, and a prosperous-looking cow. The round window at the East End of the Nine Altars was taken down, and the mason told to replace it with an exact copy, but he preferred to exercise his own ingenuity in what he believed to be improvements. All this stirred great indignation in John Carter, who visited the cathedral in 1795 and made a set of careful drawings which he published in 1801. In a series of letters to the *Gentlemen's Magazine*, which ran from December 1801 to June 1802, he described the building as he found it and castigated the so-called improvements which were taking place. Carter was a resolute critic of Wyatt and his kind and tireless in exposing their vandalism.

## 3
## SENSE AND SENSIBILITY IN 1804

The chapter was now ready to do something to the central tower and turned for guidance to a new architect, W. Atkinson, a pupil of Wyatt, who afterwards completed Abbotsford for Sir Walter Scott. In his report, dated 1804, he offered 'a few observations' on what had already been done, which show that the romantic revival was beginning to affect the taste in buildings.[17] He condemned the chipping away of the exterior which had been going on, and recommends that instead, the eroded stones should be made up with Parker's Cement. This, he explains, is a particularly useful composition, which is made just outside London, and consists of 'calcarious earth, alumine, iron and manganese'. It can be used for statuary, being very easy to carve while still soft, and sets to a tremendous hardness, and is extremely durable. Any visitor to the cathedral will agree with him there, for it has been pushed into holes all over the cathedral, and is still there as hard and as obvious as ever. One of its virtues was that it was of that 'sad sub-fuscious colour' recommended by Mr Burke in his *Essay on the Sublime and Beautiful* as adding greatly to the sublimity of buildings. The previous habit of whitewashing the cathedral was wrong. 'A large space of plain colour gives the idea of baldness and monotony, while the varied tints of natural stone never fail to provide a rich, and pleasing, effect.' The practice of painting a large black space round monuments, which had been done at Durham through the ignorance of workmen, was much to be deprecated, and such patches should be removed at once. The extra accommodation in the choir, which Wyatt had proposed to supply by extending it to the East Wall of the Nine Altars, Atkinson said could be found by building galleries at the back of the prebends' stalls, for about twenty persons each and painting them stone colour. The work on the tower was done with the cement he valued so highly, but this was too expensive and had to be stopped. About sixty years later it was all taken off.[18] In 1808 Mr Atkinson was brusquely dismissed. He was a protégé of Bishop Barrington who had found him working as a carpenter in Bishop Auckland and arranged tuition for him under James Wyatt. Barrington was in the great tradition of the see and did a good deal of building. He was a leading educationalist, a pioneer of co-operatives, and forward in all plans for helping the poor. He was a man of immense generosity and a noble patron of art and literature. The tale, so often told, of his imprisoning recalcitrant miners in his stables, is hardly fair to him. The men, who were on strike and had been turned out of their houses, had been living in tents on the open hillside. When they were arrested by the magistrates, all the gaols were full, and it was the duty of the Prince Bishop's officers to find accommodation for them, where they could. Barrington's memorial by Chantrey is in the cathedral under the central tower.

Occupied as they were with so much building, the chapter were not unmindful of other things. In 1793 they led the way in the establishment of an infirmary, which was opened on 17 September. Dr Dampier, one of the prebendaries and dean of Rochester, preached 'an excellent sermon' and a collection of £54 6s 7d was taken at the door. A procession, which included the Bishop, the Dean, and the prebendaries; as well as the Mayor and corporation, local gentry, and clergy, and 'many of the respectable inhabitants of Durham' proceeded to the building, and naturally dined together afterwards.[19] The jubilee of George III's coronation, kept on 25 October 1809, was celebrated by a collection for the benefit of poor families, and the chapter appropriated 'a large sum for the liberation of prisoners confined for small debts'.[20] When the allies took Paris in 1814, the fountain in the college was 'tastefully decorated with coloured lamps' and the cathedral bells 'rang a merry peal' as a signal for the whole town to start its illuminations.[20]

With the outburst of discontent which followed the close of the Napoleonic Wars the chapter was in bad odour in the county. Whig politics were strong there, and the prebendaries were mainly Tory. On 18 August 1821, the *Durham Chronicle*, a local paper, attacked them because they had not allowed the cathedral bells to be tolled on the death of Queen Caroline; asserting that in their politics, particularly, they 'had lost all semblance to ministers of religion'. The row took on national proportions. The Bishop prosecuted the printer, who was found guilty of libel; but a more effective defence was undertaken by Henry Phillpotts, who had formerly held a prebend and was to hold one again, but at that time had exchanged cathedral office for Stanhope, the richest living in England. With a corrosive style and a limitless supply of vitriolic invective capable of piercing the toughest skin, Phillpotts attacked the printer, his supporters, and the *Edinburgh Review*, which had taken up the cause.[21] Then, and throughout his long and contentious life, there were few people who cared to stand up to him.

In spite of all that they had done, the chapter still found that the cathedral was anything but comfortable. On their usual principle that if advice had to be taken, it had better be that of the most distinguished person possible, they asked Sir Humphrey Davy to suggest a method of heating. He was not very successful apparently, for the subject crops up again more than once in the chapter minutes. In 1802, for no known reason, they pulled down the old revestry, which stood on the South Side of the choir and was the place where the body of St Cuthbert had lain after its examination by the King's commissioners at the Reformation. The want of it has been felt ever since. Some of its stained glass was sold by the workmen and the rest destroyed. A little later this would not have been allowed to happen, for in 1816 James Raine, a scholar devoted to the Durham antiquities, became the dean and chapter's Librarian.

# 4
# OPENING ST CUTHBERT'S TOMB

Probably under Raine's influence, it was decided to open the tomb of St Cuthbert, to ascertain, if possible, whether it did indeed contain the body of the saint. There was a persistent tradition among Roman Catholics that at some time towards the end of Queen Mary's reign, it had been removed and another body substituted. Accordingly, on 17 May 1827, it was opened in the presence of two of the prebendaries, Dr Darnell, who had been John Keble's tutor at Oxford, and Dr Gilly, who had just made England aware of the plight of the Waldenses; James Raine himself; and a number of cathedral officials and workmen.[22] When they moved the great slab of Frosterley marble, which had been used to close the burial place in 1542, they found about eighteen inches of soil lying on another stone, which, from an inscription on it, had been the grave cover of Richard Haswell, a fifteenth-century monk. Below this was a pit, lined with stone, about seven feet long, four wide, and four or five deep. It had been carefully built, and was quite dry; though one end showed some roughness in the masonry, which was explained as having been left by the supports used, when the heavy slab which sealed the grave had been lowered into its place.

At the bottom of the pit and almost filling it, was a large and most decayed wooden coffin. When this was taken away, another more decayed coffin appeared, which looked as if it had once been wrapped in hide. This was thought to be the one which the monks had opened first in 1104. Heaped together at the end of it were a good many human bones, which they supposed to be the relics of saints, formerly in the feretory, and got rid of in this way when the shrine was destroyed. When these had been cleared away, yet another even more decayed coffin appeared, apparently the original coffin in which St Cuthbert's body had been placed at Lindisfarne. When it had ultimately been pieced together as well as its fragmentary condition allowed, it was seen to have on it lightly-cut figures and symbols of the saints, which were described as adorning the inner coffin when it had been opened in 1104.

Within it was a skeleton, wrapped in a linen covering, and beneath that, layer after layer of coloured and patterned silks, five different wrappings in all. There was also an ivory comb, a portable altar cased in silver, and a small linen bag like those used for holding the Blessed Sacrament. Underneath all the coverings, actually on the breast of the skeleton itself, was a small cross of gold and cloissonné work with a garnet in the centre, such as might have been St Cuthbert's pectoral cross, undisturbed since his death. There were also a superb stole, maniple, and girdle of English embroidery, which had been presented to St Cuthbert's shrine by King Athelstan, when he was at Chester-le-Street in 934. All these things were taken from the tomb and, together with some fragments of the wrappings and pieces of the original coffin, are now displayed in the dean and chapters' library. It is a pity that the examination was not delayed for another hundred years, when scientific methods would have preserved so much more. Within the coffin was another full-grown skull, which was taken to be that of King Oswald.

Though the examination of the tomb was not carried out with the skill that would have been used today, it served to show how improbable was the tradition of a substituted body. It is unlikely that if a substitution had taken place, the corpse of St Cuthbert would have been completely stripped, or if stripping had been carried out, so precious a relic as the cross would have been put on the substituted body. There was nobody who could know if they took it.

When the grave was opened again in 1899 and the bones were submitted to medical examination, they tallied exactly with what is known of St Cuthbert, as well as showing some indications that the body had once existed in a mummified state. The origin of the legend is understandable. A depressed minority would find great comfort in the thought that they alone knew the secret of the cathedral. Wishes and possibilities could so easily become facts in their eyes, but the historian cannot now accept them. There were two versions of the tradition; according to the one in lay keeping, which was revealed in 1867, the saint was buried under the steps of the tower, though an examination of them showed that they had never been disturbed; the other, said to be in the hands of the Benedictines, has never been disclosed. On 27 May 1831, the saint's feast day, Bede's grave also was examined and the remains of a human skeleton in a full-sized coffin were found three feet below the floor. An iron ring, gilded, which was on a finger bone, was removed and is now in the chapter library.

## 5
## FOUNDING THE UNIVERSITY

In the first half of the nineteenth century the old order in Church and State was breaking down. Improvements in agriculture, encouraged in the county by Bishop Barrington, and the growth of lead and coal mining had brought enormous wealth to the cathedral and the see. The deanery, which in 1788 was worth £2000 a year, was worth £9000 by 1840. Most of the prebendal incomes had increased in the same proportion, and their holders had other preferment also. The dean, Dr Jenkinson, was bishop of St David's; of his colleagues Gray was bishop of Bristol, Summer of Chester, and Phillpotts of Exeter; they claimed, when they chose to justify this situation, that it was a rough and ready re-distribution of church money, which was essential if the poorer sees were to be made economically possible; but no doubt they were, in reality, accepting a situation which had been common with their predecessors. However, the agitation for the great Reform Act of 1832 brought the whole situation under criticism. As soon as they had settled the alarming political situation, the government would be bound to notice it and might take drastic action.

For some time the old desire for a university in the North had been gaining strength. The growing population and rapidly increasing prosperity of the area, the distance from Oxford and Cambridge, and the tradition of Cromwell's college all pointed in the same direction. Just who produced the actual suggestion that the dean and chapter should found such a university is uncertain; several people are credited with it, including with some likelihood the Archbishop of Canterbury, but probably there were a number who had the same idea. However that might be, there is no doubt that the key figure in the preliminary planning and in all the early years was Charles Thorp, who in 1831 became archdeacon of Durham.[23] He was a man with a passion for work, a model parish priest at Ryton, where he succeeded his father when he was only twenty-four and where he stayed for the rest of his life, in spite of all his other offices. He was a pioneer of Sunday Schools in the North-East and the founder of the first savings bank there; he built vicarages and churches in many places throughout the diocese and was always careful to put his name somewhere about them. Besides restoring the chapel on the Inner Farne Island, he was in advance of his time in wishing to preserve the wild life there, and obtained the appointment of a warden to guard against its destruction. Busy as he was with so many other interests, education was always his most absorbing care.

The first move towards setting up the university came in a letter, dated 31 August 1831, from the dean to three prebendaries, Thorp, Durel, and Prosser. In it he said that he was anxious to increase the usefulness of the collegiate body to the public, and in order to do so, with the consent of the Bishop and the approbation of the Archbishop, he intended to bring before the chapter at the September audit, a scheme relating to an enlarged system of education. It is likely that Thorp was behind this move, for on the same day the Dean wrote to him personally, asking whether the other prebendaries who would be at the audit and had not been told of the plan, should be informed of it; if not, he was afraid that they might be jealous. He also consulted Thorp about some of the details. He need not have been anxious, for at their meeting on 28 September, the chapter unanimously approved the idea.[24] There was a good deal of discussion about financing any enlarged educational work of this kind, but the Dean was asked to inform the two Archbishops, and the Prime Minister, of their willingness to undertake it.

Thorp had already done a good deal of thinking, and there is a draft scheme of his, dated September 1831, in which he outlined specific proposals. He wanted to have a building on Palace Green with accommodation for a vice-principal and forty students. Teaching

86

space was to be found in the cathedral itself. The Galilee could become the divinity school, the dormitory lecture rooms, the crypt a hall, the exchequer a museum, and the chapter house, properly restored, be used for public occasions. The Nine Altars would be the university chapel.[25] It is interesting to speculate what the future development of the cathedral and the university would have been if this scheme had been put into operation. No notice, however, was taken of it, though the general idea of a university progressed. The bishop, Van Mildert, gave enthusiastic support, but questioned the wisdom of overpaying the professors, in case they should look on their posts as sinecures and find subordinates to do their work. Some members of the chapter had doubts and reservations from early on; others thought that it was all very well, but they were spending too much money on it, and that more of their surplus funds should go to the augmentation of poor livings. This last argument Thorp dealt with, by pointing out that the chapter had absorbed for general purposes funds which had belonged to Durham College, Oxford, until the Reformation, and which successive governments had always intended should be used for higher education in Durham; to use them for that purpose now was not to rob other church causes. After a good deal of argument finance was gradually straightened out. On his part, the Bishop agreed to appropriate three stalls, make an outright gift of £1000, and a yearly grant of £1000, which he would eventually double; and allow the use of a house near Durham Castle, which was his personal property, for as long as he was bishop. On their part, the chapter agreed to enfranchise their South Shields estate, which was valued at £80,000 and would bring in £3000 a year.

On 10 December 1831, the Dean informed the chapter that Thorp had been provisionally appointed warden of the new university, and later in the same month, Thorp produced a sketch of what he thought the staff should be to deal with all the subjects then taught in a university. Meanwhile, the necessary legislation was being piloted through the House of Lords by the Bishops, and through the Commons by Sir James Scarlett. There was some discussion about whether nonconformists should be allowed to take degrees, or if degrees should be restricted to members of the Church of England, as at Oxford and Cambridge. This was the case in the end, though nonconformists were given permission to attend the lectures if they wished. On 4 July 1832, less than a year after the scheme was first mooted, it received the Royal Assent.

87

The first students were accepted in the Michaelmas Term 1833. Accommodation was found for them in various places. A large house on Palace Green known as Archdeacon's Inn, which the chapter had just sold, was bought back again and used to house the men under the care of the bursar. The old song school, the writing school, and the almshouses on Palace Green, which went back to Bishop Cosin's time, were handed over for lecture rooms, and the alms-folk housed elsewhere. In 1837 the Ecclesiastical Commissioners, at the suggestion of the Dean and with the consent of the Bishop, gave Durham Castle as a college for the students, and it has since been known as University College.[26] Durham School, which the chapter had always maintained and carried on in a building just outside the cathedral churchyard, was moved in 1842 to a site across the river; the premises thus vacated were used as a divinity school. On 20 July 1834 a Royal Charter authorizing a Senate and a Convocation for the new university was granted and supplemented by another in 1837. So Durham ran neck and neck with London as the first university to be established in England since the Reformation.

Ultimate control rested with the bishop as visitor, and the dean and chapter as governors, with the ongoing business managed by the warden, the senate, and convocation. Thorp was both warden of the university and master of University College. In all the difficulties that arose he was consulted and he was generally the decisive voice in their solution as well as the shaper of policy. In the early days he suggested a scheme for a department of education for training schoolmasters in connection with the university, an idea which was well in advance of his time; and when this fell through, he promoted in 1839 the institution which developed into Bede College. Thorp was unquestionably the dominant figure in all the early years of the university. At the turn of the century old men still remembered him in his silk gown and velvet cap, 'a bright, cheery, kindly, and dignified old gentleman, with more than a touch of the Northumbrian burr in his utterance'.[27]

For a while the new university was fashionable in the North. Three sons of noblemen and eight sons of baronets were at University College 'about 1840'.[28] A fair number of men came from the older universities to study theology under Dr Jenkyns, the professor of theology, who was one of the ablest teachers of his day. But times changed. The spread of railways and the liberalization of Oxford and Cambridge attracted students to those places who might otherwise have gone to Durham. As Thorp grew older, he became even

88

more dictatorial. Good teachers left and fewer students came. The old man's long reign was ending in disaster. There was a shortage of funds. It had been hoped that the great families and industrialists of the wealthy North would be generous, but they were not. The cathedral remained, with the bishop, the university's only benefactor of importance, until public money became available at the beginning of the twentieth century. A Royal Commission, which sat in 1862, and a new warden introduced changes, which helped to make the university viable again.

<h1 style="text-align:center">6</h1>

# REARRANGEMENT AND RENEWAL

In 1831, while the whole project for a university was still being shaped, the Ecclesiastical Commissioners had come into existence, to inquire into the revenues and patronage of the Church of England. In their first report, issued on 19 March 1835 the bishop of Durham was deprived of his status as a Prince Palatine, and his income reduced from what it had been, which nobody quite knew, to £7000 a year. Their second report, issued on 4 March 1836, dealt drastically with cathedral chapters. The days of the old sinecure prebendaries were over. Some of them had not even bothered to perform the minimum of duties attached to their office. They remained, mute evidence of the fact that some relative had once held the bishoprick of Durham. Francis Egerton, the ninth and last Earl of Bridgewater, had been appointed to the Fourth Stall by his brother in 1780. He lived in Paris until his death in 1829, unmarried, but with his house full of cats and dogs, who were dressed as ladies and gentlemen, taken for airings in his carriage, and fed at his table. He left a large collection of manuscripts to the British Museum, £8000 for the best work on the 'Goodness of God as Manifested in Creation', and an illegitimate daughter.[29] There were others who were less picturesque and even less useful. The Durham chapter was now to consist of a dean and six canons, two of whom were to be professors in the university. All other titles were done away. Instead of holding separate estates, each was to receive a fixed salary, the canons £1000 a year, the dean double that amount, and on the first vacancy he was to become warden of the university with an additional £1000 a year on that account. Much of their patronage was to be handed over to the bishop, and the revenues of the suppressed stalls and of other obsolete offices were to go to the commissioners. None of this would operate at once. The holders were secure for their lifetime, but as they fell in, the redundant prebends would not be filled, and Durham, like other cathedrals, would live under a new system.

With this transformation in sight Van Mildert died in 1836, and was buried with semi-regal pomp in front of the high altar in the cathedral; his funeral inspired a poem from F. W. Faber which was packed with nostalgia for days past. His successor was Edward Maltby, a Greek scholar, a liberal, and a friend of Brougham, who shocked the diocese by going about without the old full-bottomed wig. Four years later Bishop Jenkinson died, and there was a new dean. George Waddington came to Durham with a great reputation for wit, learning, and knowledge of the world. He was an original member of the Athenaeum, a Fellow of Trinity College, Cambridge, and a church historian of some importance in his day. As a young man of twenty-eight, who happened to be in Venice, he ran into a friend, Thomas Hanbury, who was thinking of a journey to Ethiopia; and in the casual manner of young men, the two of them decided that they would go and take a look at the upper reaches of the Nile. It was a more or less light-hearted adventure. Dressed as Turks and attended by an Irishman named James Curtin, who knew the country, a black slave who was going to meet his master, two Maltese, and a dog named Anubis after the dog-headed divinity of the ancient Egyptians, they went up the river as far as Meroe; whence they were sent back by Ismael Pasha, who was devastating the country in search of gold and slaves. Mr Moorehead, who mentions this journey in his book on *The Blue Nile*, is a little hard on Waddington. He speaks of him as 'scholarly, dilettante, elegant, a mighty indulger in his own prejudices, and often inaccurate', but gives him credit for 'a polished and amusing account of his experiences'.[30] But neither Waddington nor Hanbury were dedicated explorers. They were observant and interested young men on a vacation adventure which they hoped to write about afterwards, in the same way that other travellers were writing up their jaunts to the Near East. They neither took themselves, nor expected others to take them, with overwhelming seriousness.

When Waddington arrived in Durham, church restoration was becoming the rage all over England, and he was anxious to do something about the interior of the cathedral. He wanted, as he said, to 'utilize' the transepts and the nave, by which he probably meant that he wished the worshippers there to see what was happening in the choir. He also thought that if the whole length of the cathedral from the West Wall of the Galilee to the Neville Screen, could be taken in at a glance, the vista would be impressive. His architect was Anthony Salvin, a member of an old Durham family who was practising in London and reckoned to be the greatest authority of his time on medieval military architecture. He had carried out work on the Tower of London and Windsor Castle, as well as many other ancient buildings of importance throughout the country, and had also done a good deal for Durham University. Between them, they took down the elaborately carved seventeenth-century choir screen and placed the organ, which it had carried, between two pillars opposite the bishop's throne. They did away with the return stalls, and rearranged those of the canons, much to their detriment. The altar rails, which had been put in after the Commonwealth, were replaced by a 'series of low open niches of Caen stone with shafts of Purbeck marble and iron gates in the middle painted and gilded'.[31]

Then, to get the vista they wanted, they removed Langley's altar from the Galilee, and opened up the great West Door of the cathedral, but found the result very disappointing. The building seemed smaller, rather than larger, than it did before. To open up the cathedral still more, the screens and doors which had enclosed the choir aisles were taken away. To bring everything into harmony with what they thought a Norman building should be like, the ornate eighteenth-century pulpit was removed, and Mr Salvin designed something in stone to take its place. In the same way, the Italianate marble font, put in after the Commonwealth, was given away to a village church and its wooden canopy placed elsewhere. A square imitation-Norman affair, standing uncovered, was considered more suitable. Windows which had been put into the aisles at various times during the Middle Ages, were replaced by those of a round-headed Norman type, and one or two others altered in imitation of some in churches in Lincolnshire and elsewhere. Prior Castell's clock, which had survived the Scots' prisoners, was also considered un-Norman, so its case was taken down, and the face put level with the wall. The old oblong of scarlet quilted silk which had been above the altar, was replaced by an 'alto-relievo of Leonardo da Vinci's Last Supper in Caen stone', and the Jacobean woodwork round St Cuthbert's shrine, which was thought to be a poor affair, was taken down in order to allow a clear view of the back of the Neville Screen from the Nine Altars. It was all very regrettable, and all done with the best advice! But eminent architects reflect the taste of their time as much as other people, and that taste is always considered to be superior to all others, which it rarely is.[32]

Waddington was a popular dean. His stately presence, greatly enhanced as he grew older, by a fine head of snow-white hair, his sonorous voice, and fine delivery were most impressive. He particularly enjoyed preaching to the school, and many of his sermons, straightforward affairs not overburdened by religious subtleties, were printed at the request of the boys. He remained a man of George IV's time, when gentlemen cultivated their idiosyncrasies. Pugilism had been fashionable in his younger days, and when he was old he still visited the boxing booths at Durham races, and was not above taking a turn himself. He never married, but had his two sisters keeping house for him. His stock of wine was superb, and the ritual of the dining table strictly observed; he once rebuked one of Her Majesty's judges for coming late to dinner. He would allow no pictures in his dining room, except those of fruit and birds. A strong Whig, with a chapter which was equally stubborn in its Toryism, he once had John Bright to stay with him, much to their disgust. Puseyism he abominated, and he would invite people whom he suspected of such leanings to a particularly lavish meal on Ash Wednesday or some other solemn fast day. Durham, which loves a character, took him to its heart.[33]

The report of the Cathedrals Commission of 1854 showed that the suggestions of the Ecclesiastical Commissioners were slowly working out. There were now a dean and nine canons, three of whom would not be replaced. There were six minor canons, ten lay vicars, and ten choristers. In all there was a total of 139 offices still connected with the cathedral, of which nine were due to disappear. Mattins and Evensong were sung every day, and there was a service on Sunday evenings during the summer. In 1822 there was still an early morning service, at six-thirty in the summer and seven o'clock in the winter, and the sung service at ten o'clock in the morning and at four in the afternoon; but by the time of this report, the early service had disappeared, though the others were still at the former times.[34] There was a sermon every Sunday and another in the choir on special days, and a sermon in the Galilee on Sunday evenings. Holy Communion was celebrated every Sunday after the morning service, and at a similar time on Christmas Day and Holy Thursday; frequently it was sung. With minor changes, the picture of cathedral worship was still very much what it was at the end of the seventeenth century.

The chapter reported that the fabric was now in good repair, the income from the woods, mines, and quarries still being devoted to that purpose, though it was often insufficient. Large gifts were made to charity which, though not specifically reported to the commissioners, included the setting up of elementary schools throughout the diocese.[35] They still maintained the grammar school, gave one hundred pounds a year to the college for training schoolmasters, and augmented poor livings. All together the chapter was just paying its way, the total income for 1852 being £57,801 13s 2¼d, the expenditure £57,800 13s 9½d. Accounting could hardly be more careful! These sums were more than double those of any other cathedral in England, except Westminster Abbey, which had just over half as much.

In 1849 the prebendal house of the Fifth Stall, which had been made out of the South End of the monastic dormitory, was pulled down, and the whole of that great room turned into a library. It was done under the supervision of Mr Philip Hardwick, who had designed many important buildings including the old Euston Station, and took four years to complete. Much of the walls was rebuilt, the windows redesigned, and a new floor laid in which the marble centre walk, still there when Carter came in 1795, disappeared. The massive roof-beams were left untouched. The appointment of William Greenwell, one of the first graduates of the university, as dean and chapter librarian in 1862, brought a first-rate medievalist to the care of their muniments and their collection of books now numbering 522 manuscript volumes, 11,000 printed works (which have vastly increased in number since), and many important private papers. Greenwell was an inveterate collector. At one time or another he presented a great number of objects from ancient barrows to the British Museum, a collection of skulls to Oxford University, added to the group of sculptured stones in the dean and chapter library, sold an important collection of stone implements to another enthusiast, and still retained a unique assemblage of gold and bronze objects, which he had dug out of ancient barrows. Anglers know him as the inventor of Greenwell's Glory, a particularly seductive fly.[36]

In 1859 the cement which Atkinson had put on part of the central tower was falling away, and a fresh restoration was undertaken with the advice of Sir Gilbert Scott. Buttresses which had been pared away were thickened, the surface renewed with stone, the old statues put back and new ones made to fill the remaining niches. Some people complained that the general aspect of the tower was altered in the process. Waddington's last days were filled with important work. In 1862 Thorp, broken-hearted at the evidence given to the university commission, at last resigned; and Waddington succeeded him and though he was too old to make all the changes required, brought some new life to the university. He died in 1869, the first dean since the seventeenth century to make Durham his home.

He was succeeded by William Charles Lake in both his offices. Lake had been a distinguished tutor of Balliol College and a member of a number of important commissions on education; with the needs of the university in mind, he was a good choice. Under his leadership theological colleges, both at home and overseas, were brought into contact with Durham; some faculties, which for one reason or another, had not proved viable, were transferred to Newcastle. More students began to arrive and the university took an upward turn. Lake persuaded the chapter to give financial support to the College of Science in Newcastle, which has since developed into the university. He believed enthusiastically in the Scottish system of education, and hoped for something like it in Newcastle. With that in mind he gave all the help he could to the College of Science there, which looked back to him as 'its real founder'.[37]

Lake had been brought up under Arnold at Rugby and reflected the earnestness of the mid-Victorians as much as Waddington had done the easier ways of the early years of the century. He came to Durham well aware of the powers of the dean, and determined to exercise them; for, in his opinion, many changes were needed in its way of life. Technically there was nothing much wrong with the music. However neglectful they had been in other ways, the chapter had always given that most careful attention. The singing men were well paid and practice was encouraged by a payment of 7s for each attendance. When needed, special teaching was provided for both vocal and instrumental music. The boys were from the city and lived at home. They were paid sums from £17 to £27 a year, given a simple education, and when their voices broke, apprenticed at the chapter's expense. The personal problems of the choirmen were not overlooked; when in November 1786 one of them, a Mr Banks, was attacked by a highwayman, he was given the money to prosecute him. In January 1847 Mr Matthew Brown, who was a key man in the choir for a very long time, was given a fortnight's leave of absence, and £20 'to defray the expense of a set of teeth and of his journey to London for that purpose'.[38] The organist seems to have had little to do with the training of the choir, which was mainly in the hands of the precentor, who must have done his work well, for when, in 1840, William Howitt visited Durham on one of his book-producing expeditions, he wrote of 'the masterly chanting in the cathedral, perhaps unrivalled in the empire'.[39] From 1849 to 1862 the precentor was Dr J. B. Dykes, the writer of so many well-known hymn tunes. His sympathies were Tractarian, and he did his best to induce more seemly behaviour. The choir were no longer brought within the altar rails when they sang the Communion Service, but stayed in their stalls. The boys were made to enter the church in an orderly procession, instead of helter-skelter, but the men refused to co-operate.[40]

The increased reverence which Dykes tried to instil, but without much help from the authorities, was very much to the mind of Lake. He always retained 'a vivid recollection of his horror' when he first saw the singing men coming one by one into the choir, buttoning up their surplices as they hurried up the nave. From then on they robed in the vestry and entered in procession, in spite of their indignation. On Sunday afternoons visitors had strolled about the church, waiting to listen to the anthem, a practice he refused to tolerate. The Holy Communion had always been celebrated at midday but he insisted that it should be at eight o'clock in the morning, not only on Sunday but on every holy day as well, and that there should be a sung Celebration once a month. Afternoon sermons were introduced in Advent and Lent, with distinguished preachers from outside being invited. Swarms of sightseers wandering about the building made it impossible for anybody who wanted to say his prayers to find a little quiet. Lake therefore restored the Gregory Chapel at his own expense to make that possible.[41]

From the beginning Lake was dissatisfied with the interior of the cathedral, and wished to change it. The chapter supported him unanimously, and in 1870 Sir Gilbert Scott was invited to direct the work. The cathedral had to be partially closed while it was being done, but the daily services were continued all the time. Baring, then bishop of Durham, was strongly against what was proposed; whether he wanted the money used elsewhere, or was just against it being spent, is not clear; but he described it as 'unwise, lavish, and wasteful'. Probably he put it down as another result of the Tractarianism he so much disliked. Some of the canons were a little shaken by this opposition, but Lake was not the man to be frightened off when he intended to do something. The whitewash which had been plastered all over the church throughout the centuries was scraped off, and the beauty of the stonework seen once more. A large wooden altar to encase the marble one which Dean Hunt had put in was made for the East End; the stone niches, which Salvin had erected for communicants, were replaced by a brass altar rail; and Salvin's pulpit, an undistinguished affair, was removed. As sermons were now to be preached in the nave, instead of the choir, the present ornate marble pulpit 'of Lombardic type' was placed in the crossing. Opposite to it, Scott installed a replica of the brass lectern which had been in use in medieval times, a pelican feeding her young, decorated with rock crystal and amethyst. In the choir, the stalls were restored and placed in something like their original position, though of course it was impossible to bring back the return stalls, and the whole of the choir was repaved with coloured marble. Above the altar a dorsal of cloth of gold replaced Salvin's copy of the Last Supper; and the ladies of the diocese subscribed to buy a silver-gilt cross, the first to be on the altar since the Reformation. But the chief glory of the new work, and one which could not be sufficiently admired, was the Choir Screen, which Sir Gilbert Scott designed to break the vista which Waddington and Salvin had sought to achieve, and which proved so disappointing. Everybody acclaimed it as 'aesthetically perfect'.[42] Whether it is or not any visitor to the cathedral can judge for himself, as it is still there.

In 1876 the work was finished, and the cathedral reopened, with a series of services and eminent preachers. Bishop Baring refused to have anything to do with it, but nearly four hundred clergy of the diocese, and 'a thousand people of every class' were present, and there were five hundred communicants at the early Celebration. The renovated cathedral still had a chilly look to Lake and his friends; he therefore launched an appeal for stained glass, and collected enough money to fill all the principal windows in the Nine Altars and the South Aisle. The lovely glass in the great West Window had been put in by Waddington. The Galilee, which the university used for their morning prayers, needed attention. The registry, which had been there for the greater part of its history, was found a place on Palace Green, and the whole building cleaned and renovated. By the time that all this had been done, the cathedral, in its main features, had taken on the appearance which it has today. Every hundred years or so the Church seems to feel the need to change its public aspect. The movement which produces this may be of slow growth, but the alteration appears to take place within a few years, and extends not only to organization and to the arrangement of church interiors, but even to the dress of the clergy. Behind it lies a changed theological emphasis. Lake, and those who were doing similar things elsewhere, were inspired by a renewed sacramentalism.

The death of Bishop Lightfoot in 1889 offered an occasion for restoring the Norman Chapter House in his memory, which was done under the supervision of Charles Hodgson Fowler. An appeal for funds was well supported, and what Wyatt had destroyed was restored as nearly as possible to what it had been in the twelfth century, though it was not completed in Lake's time. He would have liked to fill the empty niches in the Neville Screen with figures similar to those which had been there originally, but this time the chapter would not agree. Canon H. B. Tristram, a traveller and naturalist, who had got together a famous collection of stuffed birds by the simple expedient of giving any missionary who was proceeding overseas a small gun, and telling him to shoot any interesting-looking birds and send the skins to him, led the opposition. A staunch supporter of Reformation principles, he said that if the project went forward he would be compelled, next time it was his turn to preach, to read the *Homily Against the Peril of Idolatry, and Superfluous Decking of Churches*, and he must warn his brethren that he had read it through to his wife the night before, and it had taken one hour and a half. The idea was dropped.[43]

In his report to the Cathedrals Commission of 1885, Lake had said that it was still the precentor's duty to keep a record of services, and of the attendances of major and minor canons, as it had been in Cosin's time.[44] His books show that things were not always conducted with the punctuality and dignity which Lake desired, and that the Dean was sometimes an offender himself. Canon Evans, the professor of Greek, a very absent-minded man, was in the habit of forgetting what was going on and casually wandering off; a proceeding which on 24 November 1883 the precentor felt could only be adequately described in the words which Cicero applied to Catiline, 'Excessit, evasit, erupit' (He escaped, evaded, eluded us). The tale goes that on one occasion when he was being led out to preach, he was so engrossed in thought that he walked past the pulpit and went home. Other canons also had their ways. Canon Farrar, the professor of divinity, is frequently absent when in close residence, or 'strolls in late'. On Advent Sunday 1882 he never appeared until the end of the service, which was left entirely to the precentor; and the visiting preacher 'had to take care of himself'. Canon Tristram occasionally 'blustered in in the middle of the psalms', and the absence of Canon Body, a well-known mission preacher, gives an opportunity for a little word-play; the precentor wrote, 'One Body due, No Body present' and on the evening of the same day, 'No Body, or other Major Substance, present'. The Dean's frequent absences or late appearances (on one occasion he did not turn up until after the sermon), are recorded by the precentor in large letters, followed by several exclamation marks.[45] The Victorians were not quite as punctilious as we sometimes think.

Lake resigned in 1894 and died three years later at Torquay. He was shy, masterful, austere, and lacking the sympathy which would have made his contacts with other people so much easier. His Tractarianism, which grew more pronounced as time went on, rendered him less than congenial to his bishop in Baring's day, though he was a friend of Lightfoot, and had some influence on his decision to accept the bishoprick of Durham. He enjoyed pastoral work in those cases where he was certain that his help would be accepted by the people concerned, but the insomnia from which he suffered could make him irritable with his daily associates.[46] He was a Liberal in politics and a life-long friend of Gladstone; but though anxious to do good to all sorts of people, he never quite saw himself on a level with them. He felt himself to be a superior man and was unable to hide his conviction.

Much has happened since Lake's day. A large part of the wealth which formerly belonged to the cathedral has now passed into the hands of the Church Commissioners, and serves the purposes of the Church throughout England. Since 1966 the chapter has worked under a new and simpler set of statutes, which none the less preserve something of the spirit of the old. The dean is no longer warden of the university which, since 1909, has had a chancellor and vice-chancellor of its own and has in every way fulfilled the highest hopes of its founders. Work on the fabric of the cathedral goes on continually. Some of the devastation of Waddington and Salvin has been restored. The seventeenth-century font, for instance, has been brought back, and the imitation Norman affair got rid of. The woodwork surrounding St Cuthbert's shrine has been replaced; a good deal of it had been used in the university library and was generously given back. Prior Castell's great clock has been rebuilt in its former position, and as much of the original woodwork as could be recovered included in the reconstruction. Owing to the great weight which rests on the centre piers of the bell tower, the outer and inner skin of the wall had split apart, leaving great cavities. In 1922 Mr W. D.

Caroe was called in to remedy this, which he did by tying the whole tower together with stiffening beams and inserting concrete bonders.[47] In 1924 he designed a memorial chapel for the Durham Light Infantry, to occupy the place in the South Transept where the altar of Our Lady of Bolton had formerly stood. His design was influenced by 'suggestions from Lady Sybil Eden'. The cost, £1390, was found by the regiment, the dean and chapter, and private subscription.[48] The chapel has been considerably altered since. Recognition of the debt owed to the mining community has been made by the erection of a memorial to all those who have lost their lives in the pits. It is of Spanish and English seventeenth-century woodwork assembled to a design by Donald McIntyre. An important piece of modern work is the memorial in the Galilee Chapel to Dean Alington by Mr George Pace, who has also refitted the ancient spendiment or treasury to house rare books and manuscripts. Every year on their gala day more than two thousand miners and their families follow their bands into the cathedral. The music of the brass, filling the vast building with noble sound, and the great crowd of worshippers make it one of the most moving occasions of the year. The Methodists come for their Big Meeting every summer and many other associations for their own occasions throughout the year. In 1967 Her Majesty Queen Elizabeth II honoured the cathedral by distributing her Royal Maundy there.

All cathedrals today are entering a new phase in their history. There are undoubted problems but also great opportunities. The sheer cost of maintenance in days of ever rising prices is one of the great difficulties. An expensive fabric has to be kept in good condition. Organists and choristers, who continue the superb tradition of English church music which it would be an incalculable loss to let die, have to be suitably rewarded for their skill. Vergers and craftsmen must all be properly paid. All this may seem to be beyond the resources of some cathedrals, and there may be a temptation to give it up as too demanding. But that would be to fail in a unique ministry. Perhaps the State may help, as the coming together of different religious traditions brings the cathedrals more into use by all Christian people. But, as we have seen in many cases already, there is a great fund of goodwill in large sections of the public which will, no doubt, assist in meeting the needs. But at any cost the spiritual purposes for which the cathedrals were built must not be forgotten, and these great churches allowed to degenerate into museums—dead examples of the art and architecture of former ages.

They must continue to maintain, as they have done in the past, a high standard of worship, and one in which the people of today can most readily take part. The daily offices, morning and afternoon, testify to prayer as a vital part of man's being, which must not be pushed into a corner, but which is of, at least, equal importance to the practical work of the day. Casual visitors, dropping in at these times as they do, encounter something which is for many of them a new dimension of life. The vast hordes of sightseers, which modern holiday habits bring to the cathedrals, offer a point of contact with multitudes who would never be reached in any other way. Many welcome a personal ministry, and a friendly approach, if only in the first place to explain something of interest, can lead to deeper usefulness. The building itself, instinct with living worship, can hardly fail to impress on those who are moderately sensitive, that there are finer things in life than money, popular acclaim, and sensual satisfaction. In an age of increasing materialism this is not to be despised.

The cathedrals are kept in touch with public life by the attendance of local and national associations on particular occasions and by their services to the cultural activities of the neighbourhood, which is all to the good. A cathedral can be the heart of the diocese. With a long tradition of learning, and often large libraries, cathedrals can become not only a focus for the widest possible scholarship, which is more than ever necessary today, but teaching centres where old methods can be shown at their best, experiments tried, and new methods demonstrated. Three or four priests, based on the cathedral and free to move about the diocese wherever they are wanted, could do great service in those parishes which, owing to the shortage of clergy or some other cause, have to wait a long time for an incumbent. Some association of the Bishop's Council with the cathedral could assist the work of both. For everybody, clergy and laity alike, the cathedral should be the place where friendship and counsel can be found. In a rapidly changing situation a blue print for the future of all cathedrals is impossible. Differently placed, they will find different ways of service, but if we remain spiritually sensitive as new opportunities arise, the future can be even richer than the past.

# Notes

## 1

## THE MIDDLE AGES

The chroniclers, Simeon of Durham, *fl.* 1130 and his continuator; Reginald of Coldingham, *fl.* 1162; Geoffrey of Coldingham, *fl.* 1214; Robert of Greystones, *fl.* 1330; William of Chambre, *fl.* 1365 record the medieval history of the Durham abbey. Simeon of Durham's *Chronicle* is published in the Rolls Series, vol. 1 (1882), 2 (1885), both edited by T. Arnold. The works of Geoffrey of Coldingham, Robert of Greystones, and William of Chambre are published in *Scriptores Tres*, edited by James Raine, Surtees Society (1839). William Hutchinson, *The History and Antiquities of the County Palatine of Durham* (Durham 1823) and James Raine, *St Cuthbert* (Durham 1828), give large extracts from the chroniclers as well as including other documents of importance. Robert Hegg, *The Legend of St Cuthbert* (1626), edited by George Allan and privately printed at Darlington in 1777, is a period piece of great charm. John Harvey, *English Mediaeval Architects* (London 1954) has been referred to for the architects mentioned in the text down to 1550, the period covered by that book; details of some of the later architects can be found in H. M. Colvin's *Biographical Dictionary of English Architects, 1660-1846* (London 1954). Three modern studies, G. V. Scammell, *Hugh du Puiset* (Cambridge 1956), C. M. Fraser, *A History of Antony Bek* (Oxford 1957), and R. L. Storey, *Thomas Langley* (London 1961) are of great value. Any student of the History of Durham has the tremendous advantage of the Surtees Society's publications, which are referred to in their place. In the abbreviations D. & C. stands for the Dean and Chapter of Durham.

1. B. Colgrave, ed., *Two Lives of St Cuthbert* (Cambridge 1940). Latin text, ET, and notes
2. *VCH* (London 1907), vol. 2, p. 137
3. J. T. Fowler, *ed.*, *The Rites of Durham*, Surtees Soc. (1902), p. 66. The introduction contains a full account of the manuscripts and various printed editions of the *Rites*, and the notes are a mine of information. For the Hogg Roll, an early MS of the *Rites*, are D. & C. MSS CIII. 23
4. J. Raine, *St Cuthbert* (Durham 1826), p. 60
5. W. Hutchinson, *History and Antiquities of Durham* (Durham 1823), vol. 1, p. 134
6. W. Greenwell, *ed.*, *Feodarium Dunelmensis*, Surtees Soc. (1871), p. xxvii; H. S. Offler, *ed.*, *Durham Episcopal Charters*, Surtees Soc. (1968)

7. VCH, vol. 2, p. 137
8. G. M. Trevelyan, *History of England* (London 1926), p. 120
9. W. Greenwell, *Durham Cathedral* (Durham 1881), p. 34
10. H. S. Offler, *Rannulph Flambard as Bishop of Durham*, Durham Cathedral Lecture 1972, D. & C. Office
11. This was important as, together with the ring, it was the symbol that he was legally in possession of his see
12. J. T. Fowler, *ed., Rites*, p. 68
13. J. Raine, p. 199
14. Ibid., p. 74 ff
15. W. Greenwell, *Durham Cathedral*, p. 45
16. W. Hutchinson, *History*, vol. 1, p. 192
17. G. V. Scammell, *Hugh du Puiset* (Cambridge 1956)
18. Ibid., p. 94
19. Ibid., p. 92
20. J. Harvey, *English Mediaeval Architects* (London 1954), article on Elias of Dereham
21. J. Raine, p. 56 fn. 136
22. W. Hutchinson, *History*, vol. 1, p. 260
23. C. M. Fraser, *A History of Antony Bek* (Oxford 1957)
24. W. Hutchinson, *History*, vol. 2, p. 102
25. C. M. Fraser, *Antony Bek*, ch. vii, viii
26. W. Hutchinson, *History*, vol. 2, p. 111
27. J. Harvey, op. cit., article on John Lewyn
28. D. & C, MSS, *Cellarer's Accounts* 1346-7, month 8
29. R. Surtees, *History of Durham* (London 1816), vol. 1, p. 1
30. J. T. Fowler, *ed., Rites*, p. 19
31. R. Surtees, vol. iv, City of Durham, p. 6
32. J. Boyle, *The County of Durham* (London n.d.), p. 250. The mark was worth about 66p
33. J. Harvey, *Henry Yevele* (London 1944), p. 37
34. J. Harvey, *English Mediaeval Architects*, article on John Lewyn
35. W. Hutchinson, *History*, vol. 2, p. 92
36. W. Greenwell, *Durham Cathedral*, p. 99
37. *Scriptores Tres*, Surtees Soc. (1839), Middleton, p. clxxx; Dryng, p. clxxxvii
38. R. L. Storey, *Thomas Langley* (London 1961)
39. Ibid., p. 193
40. Ibid., pp. 195-6
41. W. Hutchinson, *History*, vol. 1, p. 338
42. Ibid., vol. 2, p. 12 ff
43. J. T. Fowler, *ed., Rites*. See note 3 above
44. Ibid., p. 33
45. J. Raine, p. 121
46. *Sanctuarium Dunelmense et Sanctuarium Beverlacense*, Surtees Soc. (1837). No editor mentioned but probably Temple Chevalier.
47. J. T. Fowler, *ed., Rites*, p. 10. 'Antic work' is grotesque, fantastic work. 'Candlestick metal' is latten, an alloy of copper and zinc practically indistinguishable from brass.
48. Ibid., pp. 89, 90

49. Ibid., p. 89
50. Ibid., p. 102
51. J. T. Fowler, *Durham Account Rolls*, Surtees Soc. (1898), vol. 2, p. 454
52. Nothing like this is mentioned elsewhere and it is suggested that it was a crosier. But those who opened the coffin knew perfectly well what a crosier was, and if it had been that might be expected to say so. Possibly it was a staff of dignity, put in as an offering at some unrecorded opening of the coffin; D. & C. Misc. Charters 7205 (bill for grave).
53. J. Raine, p. 174 ff
54. W. Hutchinson, *History*, vol. 2, p. 133. The original deed of surrender has disappeared. There is a late sixteenth- or early seventeenth-century copy in D. & C. Miscellaneous Charters 428. Another copy, in Bishop Cosin's hand, is in D. & C. MSS 218. Dugdale, *Monasticon* (London 1817), vol. 1, p. 231; Speed, *The History of Great Britain* (London 1627), vol. 1, p. 807

# 2
# THE REFORMATION

1. Hamilton Thompson, *The Statutes of the Cathedral Church of Durham*, Surtees Soc. (1929), p. 5
2. D. & C. Additional MS. 218
3. John Strype, *Annals of the Reformation* (London 1725), vol. 2, p. 656
4. Hamilton Thompson, *Statutes*, p. xxxvi
5. Thomas Fuller, *The Worthies of England* (London 1662), pt. 1
6. W. Hutchinson, *History*, vol. 2, p. 150
7. M. A. E. Green, ed., *Life of Mr William Whittingham, Dean of Durham*, Camden Soc. (1870)
8. Ibid., p. 12
9. John Strype, *Life of Archbishop Parker* (London 1711), vol. 1, p. 267
10. J. T. Fowler, ed., *Rites*, p. 60
11. Ibid., p. 27. It had been believed that the banner could put out fires, and could not itself be burned. Mrs Whittingham was destroying both the banner and the superstition.
12. Ibid., p. 61
13. Bernard Gilpin, *A Sermon Preached in the Court at Greenwich, Before King Edward the Sixth*, The First Sunday after Epiphany, 1552 (London 1630), p. 19. The greed of patrons, who would put anybody into their livings, provided they could get them cheap, was a universal complaint.
14. J. T. Fowler, ed., *Rites*, p. 231
15. M. A. E. Green, ed., *Mr William Whittingham*, p. 27
16. Ibid., p. 42
17. Ibid., p. 31
18. Peter Smart, *A Sermon Preached in the Cathedral Church of Durham*, 7 July 1628. (Imprinted 1628, n.p.), p. 23
19. Ibid., p. 23
20. J. T. Fowler, ed., *Rites*, p. 298
21. Peter Smart, *A Short Treatise of Altars, Altar Furniture, Altar-cringing and Music of all the Quire*—Written at the same time by Peter Smart—a little

before he was expelled. (n.p., n.d.) The preface mentions events which took place in 1641.

In the account of the cathedral given by the three soldiers referred to below (note 23) the altar is said to have cost £200 and to have been put in at the expense of Dean Hunt who had also given 'to adorne it, 2 double gilt Candelstickes, and a Bason, 2 double gilt fayre Flaggons, 2 Chalices with Covers likewise double gilt'. A *Short Survey*, p. 26

22. Cham, a form of cam, meaning wholly awry
23. A *Relation of a Short Survey of 26 Counties*—begun on August 11, 1634. By a Captain, a Lieutenant, and an Ancient. Ed. L. G. Wickham Legg (London 1904), Stuart Series, no. 7. A racy account of a visit made to the cathedral which shows how much of the medieval splendour still remained until the devastation of the Scots and the Commonwealth, including 'A font not to be paralel'd in our land, it is 8 squares, with an Iron grate, rays'd 2 yardes every square, within is a fayre ascent of diverse steps, the Cover opens like a forequarter'd Globe, the stone is of branch'd Marble, and the story is that of St John baptizing our Blessed Saviour, and the four Evangelists, curiously done, and richly painted, within the Globe all above so artificially wrought, and carv'd, with such variety of Joyners worke, as makes all the beholders thereof to admire.' p. 26. In 1663 the dean and chapter put in a new font 'somewhat suitable to that which the Scots destroyed'. Beautiful as their replacement is it falls far short of the original.
24. R. Surtees, *History of Durham*, vol. IV, City of Durham, p. 28
25. G. Ornsby, *ed., The Correspondence of John Cosin*, Surtees Soc. (1868), p. 212
26. R. Surtees, pp. 7, 10
27. J. T. Fowler, *ed., Rites*, p. 163
28. John Walker, *Sufferings of the Clergy* (London 1714), pt. 2, p. 18
29. *The Sad, and Lamentable, Case of the Tenants of the Late Dean and Chapter of Durham*. Broadsheet, D. & C. Library, I. VII.5.12
30. G. W. Kitchin, *The Seven Sages of Durham* (London 1911), p. 133; W. N. Darnell, *The Correspondence of Isaac Basire, with Memoir* (London 1831)
31. S. R. Gardiner, *History of the Commonwealth* (London 1903), vol. 1, p. 296. His account of the treatment of the prisoners hardly squares with that given in the *Rites of Durham*, pp. 14, 355
32. *Quaeries to the Master . . . of the College they are setting up at Durham, from them, in scorn, called Quakers*, Broadsheet, D. & C. Library, I.VII.11.3
33. C. E. Whiting, *History of the University of Durham* (London 1932), p. 18 ff
34. *Autobiography of Richard Baxter* (Everyman), p. 168
35. T. Zouch, *Works* (York 1820), vol. 2, p. 67
36. G. Ornsby, *ed., Miscellanea. Containing the Works and Letters of Dennis Granville*, Surtees Soc. (1861), p. 253 ff
37. Ibid., p. 261
38. R. Granville, *Life of Dean Granville* (Exeter 1902), p. 85
39. Ibid, p. 85

40. Isaac Basire, *A Funeral Sermon, together with a Brief of the Life ... of the late Lord Bishop of Durham* (London 1673)

41. Anon., *An Examination of the Life and Character of Nathaniel, Lord Crewe* (London 1790), p. 31; C. E. Whiting, *Nathaniel, Lord Crewe* (London 1940)

42. G. Ornsby, ed., *Correspondence of John Cosin*, vol. 1, p. 142. The noble was worth about 33p. 'When the Scots' armies lay here, many of the best books were carried away by them, as is known to Sir Wm Armyne, and the Commissioners of Parlt: then in the North.' Isaac Gilpin, keeper of the library, to the Durham County Committee. Feb. 4. 1650. Records of the Committee for compounding with Delinquent Royalists in Durham and Northumberland, Surtees Soc. (1905), p. 42

43. R. Granville, p. 328

44. Ibid., p. 333

45. Ibid., p. 247

46. G. Ornsby, *Miscellanea*, Surtees Soc. (1861), p. 217

47. Ibid., p. 244

48. Ibid., p. 66

49. Thomas Comber, *Memoirs of the Life and Writings of Thomas Comber*, Compiled from the original MSS (London 1799); C. E. Whiting, ed., *Memorials of Dean Comber*, Surtees Soc. (1941-2), 2 vols.

# 3
# THE EIGHTEENTH CENTURY AND AFTER

1. James Dallaway, ed., *The Letters of Thomas Rundle, Lord Bishop of Derry, in Ireland, with introductory Memoir* (Gloucester 1789). In his memoirs for 1728 John, Lord Hervey, who was at the centre of the social life of London and in a good position to know, notes how completely the upper classes had repudiated 'the fable of Christianity' and how ineffective were its apologists. See *Some Materials towards Memoirs of the Reign of King George II*, by John, Lord Hervey, ed., Romney Sedgwick (London 1931), vol. 1, p. 92

2. Samuel Weller Singer, ed., *Anecdotes, Observations, and Characters, by the Rev. Joseph Spence*; with notes and life of the author (London 1820).

3. Samuel Johnson, *Lives of the English Poets* (Everyman), vol. 2, p. 175

4. R. Straus, *Robert Dodsley* (London 1910), p. 310

5. Samuel Johnson, ibid., p. 187

6. E. Hughes, ed., *The Letters of Spencer Cowper*, Surtees Soc. (1956)

7. Ibid., p. 75

8. Ibid., p. 193

9. *Statutes of the Cathedral Church of Durham*, ch. 16. See also Appendix, p. 108

10. John Sykes, *Local Records* (Newcastle 1833), vol. 1, p. 298

11. D. & C. Minutes

12. Ibid.

13. W. Hutchinson, *History*, vol. 2, p. 402
14. D. & C. Add. MSS, 215
15. Ibid.
16. D. & C. Minutes, 20 November 1795. The suggestion to employ Wyatt probably came from James, later Earl, Cornwallis, who in 1784, added the deanery of Durham to the list of preferment he already held, which included the bishopric of Lichfield and Coventry. One of his daughters remarked at a party, 'We go to Durham for the money, and come to London to spend it'. But he could be generous. Solomon Grisdale, the curate of Merrington, who was very poor and with a large family, lost his only cow and Robert Surtees, getting up a subscription to buy him another one, approached the dean, hoping for a five-pound note at most. 'Mr Surtees,' said the dean, 'go to my steward and tell him to give you as much money as will buy the best cow you can find.' 'My Lord,' said the delighted Surtees, 'I hope you'll ride in to Heaven on the back of that cow.' *Memoir of Robert Surtees*, ed., Taylor, Surtees Soc. (1852), p. 93
17. D. & C. Add. MSS, 216
18. Atkinson's love for cement was not entirely disinterested. 'R. Smirke told me that Atkinson has a wharfe in Westminster and purchases material for cement from Lord Mulgrave, had from his Lordship's estate in Yorkshire.' Joseph Farington, *Diary* (London 1927), Entry for 18 September 1813
19. John Sykes, *Local Records* (Newcastle 1833), vol. 1, p. 368
20. Ibid., vol. 2, p. 49
21. Henry Phillpotts, 1778-1869. Held much preferment in the diocese of Durham. Bishop of Exeter, 1830, when public outcry made him exchange Stanhope for the Sixth Stall at Durham which he kept till his death. A leader in the Church and in politics, whose Tory intransigence greatly injured the bishops in public estimation. See G. C. B. Davies, *Henry Phillpotts, bishop of Exeter* (London 1954).
22. J. Raine, *St Cuthbert* (Durham 1828) gives his own detailed account of the opening. *The Relics of St Cuthbert*, ed., C. F. Battiscombe, printed for the dean and chapter, is a modern study of the relics by international experts.
23. R. Welford, *Men of Mark 'twixt Tweed and Trent* (London 1895), vol. 3, p. 523
24. C. E. Whiting, *The University of Durham* (London 1932), p. 36
25. Ibid.
26. Ibid., p. 64
27. J. T. Fowler, *The University of Durham* (London 1904), p. 112
28. Ibid., p. 101 ff
29. Joseph Farington, *Diary* (London 1927), vol. VII, p. 119 fn
30. A. Moorehead, *The Blue Nile* (London 1962), p. 173; George Waddington and Barnard Hanbury, *Journal of a Visit to some Parts of Ethiopia* (London 1822)
31. Record of Works Done, D. & C. L 942.81.p.XXXVI
32. Ibid.
33. J. T. Fowler, *University*, p. 114
34. Parson and White, *Directory of Durham and Northumberland* (Newcastle 1827), p. 172

35. *First Report of Her Majesty's Commissioners to enquire into the State, and Condition, of Cathedral and Collegiate Churches in England and Wales* (London 1854), pp. 5, 48; *Record of Benefactions made by the Dean and Chapter 1750-1857*, D. & C. 1942. 81

36. J. T. Fowler, *University* (London 1904), p. 150 ff

37. Katharine Lake, *Memorials of Dean Lake* (London 1901), p. 330. A wifely tribute bordering on hagiography

38. D. & C. Minutes, 2 January 1847. Grants to singing men in sickness, or special distress, occur with great regularity

39. W. Howitt, *Visits to Remarkable Places* (London 1856), vol. 2, p. 64

40. J. T. Fowler, *Life of Dr Dykes* (London 1897)

41. Katharine Lake, *Memorials*, p. 135

42. *Sermons at the re-opening of Durham Cathedral*, with an Introduction by G. Ornsby (London 1877), p. LXI

43. E. M. Fleming, *Memories of my Grandparents*, D. & C. Add. MSS L 942.81, pp. 8, 24

44. *First Report of Her Majesty's Commissioners for enquiring into the condition of Cathedral Churches in England and Wales*, 1882: 5, Durham, Appendix, p. 5

45. D. & C. Add. MS 5

46. Augustus Hare, *The Story of my Life* (London 1900), vol. V, p. 424, says: 'The present Dean [Lake], who has so spoilt the cathedral, is most unpopular. One day, he had taken upon himself to lecture Mr Greenwell, one of the minor canons, for doing his part in the service in thick laced boots. Greenwell was furious. Rushing out of the cathedral, he met Archdeacon Bland, the most polite and deliberate of men, and exclaimed, "I've been having the most odious time with the Dean, and I really think he must have got the devil in him." "No, Mr Greenwell, no, no, not that," said Archdeacon Bland in his quiet way; "he is only possessed by three imps; he is imperious, he is impetuous, and he is impertinent".'
    Another story tells how one of the Durham canons, who happened to be next to the Archbishop of Canterbury at dinner, was asked, "And how are things at Durham?" "Oh, very peaceful Your Grace," answered the canon. "What!" replied the Archbishop. "Don't tell me my old friend Lake is dead!"'

47. A. D. R. Caroe, *Old Churches and Modern Craftsmanship* (Oxford 1949), p. 80

48. *Durham Light Infantry Journal*, July 1934

# *Appendix 1*

## AN EIGHTEENTH-CENTURY MEAL

*The Art Of Cookery*, by John Thacker; Cook to the Honourable and Reverend, the Dean and Chapter of Durham (Newcastle 1758) gives 'A set of Bills of Fare for the Residence in the College of Durham, begun Sept. 29, 1753'. Here is the menu for the dinner for the prebendaries, set out according to the arrangement of the dishes on the table.

|  | | |
|---|---|---|
| | Soop | |
| | Remove Hanch of Venison | |
| Pudding | | Stew'd Soles |
| | Daub'd Ducks | |
| A Pulpotoon with Brochlets round | | French Peas |
| | Sturgeon | |
| Crab Loves | | Turkey and stew'd Cellery |
| | Friecandox of Veal | |
| A Leveret | | Lamb's Fry |
| | Pigeon Pye | |
| Italian Artichokes | | Mackaroney Parmasan |
| | Roast Tongue and Claret Sauce | |
| Pig | | Stew'd or scollop'd Oysters |
| | Potted Moor Game | |
| Eggs in Crampine | | Boil'd Chickens and Collyflowers |
| | Ham with Patties of Greens | |
| Mutton Cutlets marinaded | | Spinage Tart |
| | Soop | |
| | Beef, Tromblance removes | |
| | | Ruffs and Wildfowls |

# *Appendix 2*

## BISHOPS, PRIORS, AND DEANS
### BISHOPS

Aldhun 955-1018
Eadmund 1020-41
Eadred 1041-??
Aethelric 1042-56
Aethelwin 1056-71
Walcher 1071-80
William of St Carileph (Calais) 1081-96
Rannulph Flambard 1099-1128
Geoffrey Rufus 1133-40
William of St Barbara 1143-52
Hugh du Puiset 1153-95
Philip of Poitou 1197-1208
Richard Marsh 1217-26
Richard le Poor 1229-37
Nicolas Farnham 1241-48
Walter Kirkham 1249-60
Robert Stichill 1260-74
Robert of Holy Island 1274-83
Antony Bek 1284-1310
Richard Kellaw 1311-16
Lewis de Beaumont 1318-33
Richard of Bury 1333-45
Thomas Hatfield 1345-81
John Fordham 1382-88
Walter Skirlaw 1388-1406
Thomas Langley 1406-37
Robert Neville 1437-57
Laurence Booth 1457-76
William Dudley 1476-83
John Sherwood 1484-94
Richard Fox 1494-1501
William Senhouse 1502-05
Christopher Bainbridge 1507-8
Thomas Ruthall 1509-23
Thomas Wolsey 1523-29

Cuthbert Tunstall 1530-59
James Pilkington 1561-76
Richard Barnes 1577-87
Matthew Hutton 1589-95
Tobias Matthew 1595-1606
William James 1606-17
Richard Neile 1617-27
George Monteigne 1628
John Howson 1628-32
Thomas Morton 1632-59
John Cosin 1660-72
Nathaniel Crewe 1674-1722
William Talbot 1722-30
Edward Chandler 1730-50
Joseph Butler 1750-52
Richard Trevor 1752-71
John Egerton 1771-87
Thomas Thurlow 1787-91
The Hon. Shute Barrington 1791-1826
William Van Mildert 1826-36
(Last of the Palatine Bishops.)
Edward Maltby 1836-56
Charles Thomas Longley 1856-60
The Hon. Henry Montague Villiers 1860-1
Charles Baring 1861-78
Joseph Barber Lightfoot 1879-89
Brooke Foss Westcott 1889-1901
Handley Carr Glyn Moule 1901-20
Herbert Hensley Henson 1920-39
Alwyn Terrel Petre Williams 1939-52
Arthur Michael Ramsey 1952-56
Maurice Henry Harland 1956-66
Ian Thomas Ramsey 1966-72
John Stapylton Habgood 1973-

# PRIORS

Aldwin 1083-87
Turgot 1087-1109
Algar 1109-37
Roger 1137-49
Lawrence 1149-53
Absolom 1154-58
Thomas 1158-62
German 1163-86
Bertram 1188-1208
William 1209-14
Ralph Kermet 1214-33
Thomas of Melsonby 1233-44
Bertram of Middleton 1244-58
Hugh of Darlington 1258-72
Richard of Claxton 1272-85
Hugh of Darlington 1285-89

Richard of Hoton 1289-1308
William of Tanfield 1308-13
Geoffrey of Burdon 1314-22
William of Cowton 1322-41
John Fossor 1341-74
Robert of Berrington 1374-91
John of Hemmingburgh 1391-1416
John of Washington 1416-46
William of Ebchester 1446-56
John Burnaby 1456-64
Richard Bell 1464-78
Robert of Ebchester 1478-84
John of Auckland 1484-94
Thomas Castell 1494-1519
Hugh Whitehead 1524-40

# DEANS

Hugh Whitehead 1541-48
Robert Horne 1551-53
Thomas Watson 1553-57
Thomas Robertson 1557-59
Robert Horne 1559-60
Ralph Skinner 1560-63
William Whittingham 1563-79
Thomas Wilson (lay) 1580-81
Tobias Matthew 1583-95
William James 1596-1606
Sir Adam Newton (lay) 1606-20
Richard Hunt 1620-38
Walter Balcanquall 1639-45
William Fuller 1645-59
John Barwick 1660-61
John Sudbury 1662-84
Dennis Granville 1684-91
Thomas Comber 1691-99
John Montague 1699-1728

Henry Bland 1728-46
Spencer Cowper 1746-74
Thomas Dampier 1774-77
William Digby 1777-88
John Hinchcliff (bishop) 1788-94
James, Earl Cornwallis (bishop)
1794-1824
Charles Henry Hall 1824-27
John Banks Jenkinson (bishop)
1827-40
George Waddington 1840-69
William Charles Lake 1869-94
George William Kitchin 1894-1912
Herbert Hensley Henson 1912-18
James Edward Cowell Welldon
1918-33
Cyril Argentine Alington 1933-51
John Herbert Severn Wild 1951-

# Index